ROOTS

OF THE

IROQUOIS

BY

TEHANETORENS

NATIVE VOICES
SUMMERTOWN, TENNESSEE

Copyright 2000 by Tehanetorens (Ray Fadden)

Cover painting: "Ohen:ton Karihwatehkwen" which means "Words
    before all else" by David Kanietakeron Fadden
Illustrations: Kahionhes (John Fadden)
Cover design: Helios Productions
Book design: Jerry Lee Hutchens

Published by Native Voices, a division of
Book Publishing Company
P.O. Box 99
Summertown, TN 38483
1-888-260-8458

03 02 01 00   4 3 2 1

ISBN 1-57067-097-8

Tehanetorens
    Roots of the Iroquois / by Tehanetorens.
        p. cm.
    ISBN 1-57067-097-8
    1. Iroquois Indians--History. 2. Iroquois mythology. I. Title.
    E99.I7 T47   2000
    974.004'9755--dc21   00-023657

Roots of the Iroquois

Migration of the Iroquois

This story is about the Haudenosaunee, as we say in our language, or the People of the Long House, as it is translated into the English language, or the Iroquois, as the French called us, or the Six Nations, as the British called us.

Many winters in the past the Haudenosaunee lived toward the setting sun in the west. They lived where the grass grew tall and where the buffalo lived (The Great Plains). They lived beside the Great River today called the Mississippi. They dwelt near the villages of the Wolf Nation, the Pawnees. They were friends and allies of the Wolf Nation.

Northeast of their country were the Great Lakes. To the west rose the Rocky Mountains. Near the Big River, the Mississippi, were the villages of the Haudenosaunee.

For some reason, the Iroquois packed their belongings on their backs and migrated. Many footmarks led away. They headed toward the rising sun. Up the Ohio River their trail went—toward the Great Lakes, they migrated toward the rising sun.

One band went across the Great Lakes and settled on Georgian Bay. They were known as the Thastchetchi, the Huron Nation. South of them settled the Tionontati, the Tobacco People. Another band settled along the shores of Lake Erie. They were the Gaguagaono, the

Erie People. Along the Niagara River settled the Hatiwatarunh, the Neuter Nation. The Wenrohronon (Wenroe) Band settled southeast of the Neuters. Along the Susquehanna river settled the Kanastoge Nation. To the west of them, along the upper Ohio, the Honiason-tkeronon (Black Minqua) built their towns. Up the Kanawha River migrated the Nottoway and Meherrin Peoples. One band, the Oyatageronon (the Cherokee Nation) migrated far to the south across the Appalachian Mountains and settled in what is known as the Carolinas.

The main band continued down the St. Lawrence River. There they met a people who were different from them. The Haudenosaunee

noticed that when these people cooked their foods, they flavored them with different kinds of bark, so the Haudenosaunee called these people "Adirondacks" or porcupines, meaning literally, the Eaters of Bark.

The Adirondack people were smaller physically than the Haudenosaunee, but there were more of them. They were hunters, while the Iroquois were more or less farmers. The Iroquois did not get along well with the Adirondacks. Many battles were fought with the Bark Eaters. Because of this war there were many deaths. The Iroquois

were defeated by the Adirondacks. For many winters and many summers the Haudenosaunee had to pay tribute of skins and meat to the Adirondack people, who had very good warriors. Darkness (sadness) filled the hearts of the People of the Long House. But the Haudenosaunee never forgot the Creator, and they continued to

give thanksgiving to the plants, the waters, the sun, the moon, the animals, the winds. They wanted freedom, as the Eagle has. They—men, women, and children—continually spoke to the Creation and planned for freedom.

After many years of planning and with secretly stored provisions, one dark night they left their village and silently paddled their canoes up the St. Lawrence River. Their water-trail led up this river, around the Thousand Islands, toward the mouth of the Oswego River. They looked back and saw specks on the water. These distant specks were the canoes of the Bark Eaters. The Haudenosaunee knew that the Adirondacks, not being burdened with women and children, had

pursued them and would reach them before they could land.

The Adirondacks overtook the Iroquois near the mouth of the Oswego River. A great battle took place. For a time, it looked as if the Iroquois would be wiped out. The Thunder People heard their cry of distress and sent a great storm. In the confusion of the rough waters and high winds, many of the canoes of the Adirondacks overturned. Those who survived returned home.

Near the mouth of the Oswego River, the Haudenosaunee landed and erected their village. They found good hunting. They found a rich soil, good for the raising of corn, beans, and squash. For many years the home fires of the People of the Long House burned and their bark houses stood near the Oswego River. In time, they multiplied. There were many men, women, and children. The game, being used for food, became scarce.

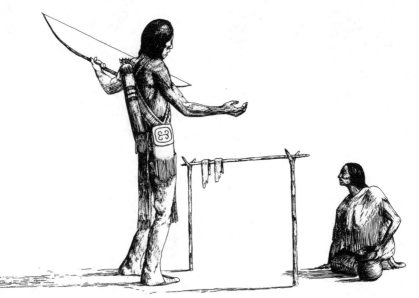

Finally, different bands of Haudenosaunee left the homeland seeking better hunting regions. They were looking for signs of deer. From their homeland along the Oswego River, their trails led south, east, and west. The Flint People, who are called the Mohawks by others, settled along the Mohawk River. Around Oneida Lake, the Standing Stone People, or Oneidas, built their villages. The People of the Hills, or Onondagas, settled along Onondaga Creek. To the west,

along Cayuga Lake, the Great Pipe People, or Cayugas, built their towns. Along Canandaigua Lake settled the People of the Great Mountain, the Senecas. Another band, the Akotaskarore or Tuscaroras, travelled far to the south. Now the one band had become six separated bands. To the east was the Hudson River, running to the sea. To the west stretched the Great Lakes. North was the St. Lawrence River and the Adirondack Mountain region and south were the Finger Lakes. In time, although related by blood, the five nations who remained in the north became enemies of each other. They forgot the ways of the Creator and fought among themselves and with others, bringing sorrow, destruction, and death to each nation.

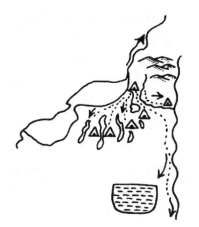

Two wise men, one whom we call today the Peacemaker, and the other, Hiawatha, organized the five nations of Long House People into a confederacy. The Peacemaker gave them a government and constitution to follow, called Kaianeregowa, or the Great Nice Way. Today we often call it "The Great Law."

The Peacemaker said, "To war against each other is foolish, as well as evil. Hunters are afraid to seek game in the forests. Fishermen fear to follow the streams. Women are afraid to work in the fields. Because of war, there is starvation, suffering, and misery. War must cease and everlasting Peace must be established among all peoples." The warriors of the Five Nations listened and thought of the words of the Wise One. They threw down their weapons of war.

The Five Nations of the People of the Long House allied themselves into one League. They compared themselves to a long bark house where there would be five fireplaces but all were of one family. The Flint People, the Mohawks, were the Keepers of the Eastern Door of that Long House. The Senecas were Keepers of the Western Door. The Onondagas, in the center, were the Fire Keepers, and theirs became the capitol of the League.

The Five Nations became as brothers again. They worked together as one people. If any one of these nations were attacked, the injury was felt by all of the Five Nations.

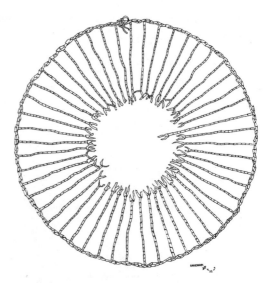

The Rotiianeson, or Nice People, whom some today call "chiefs," contributed white wampum toward a Great White Circle of Wampum. This wampum circle is the symbolic Fire of the Great Council which burns at Onondaga. It certifies the pledge words of the Rotiianeson that they will keep the unity of the Confederacy, that they are united, and form one body or League of Great Peace, which they have established. The fifty strings of wampum facing the center represent the Rotiianeson, fifty in number, the Government of the Five Nations. Each string stands for one of our leaders, and they are placed in the order in which they sit at council.

The sacred wampum belt below symbolizes the union of the Five Nations. It was made to remember the Great Peace. It means: the Five Nations are joined together by the Path of Peace. In the center is a white heart, symbolizing the Onondaga nation. It also means that the heart of the Five Nations is single in its loyalty to the Great Peace, and

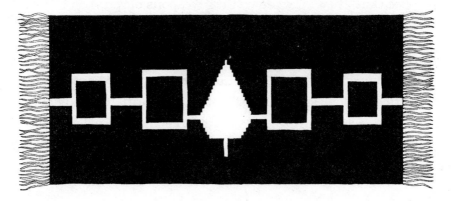

that the Great Peace is lodged in the heart, with the Onondaga people. The Peace Path extends beyond at both ends, meaning that others may follow this path and become part of the Great Peace, Kaianerekowa.

The Peacemaker said, "Our League is a Great Tree. It reaches high into the sky so that all peoples will see and know of it. The Eagle watches from its top as our guardian bird. The Tree has four white roots, White Roots of Peace that go to the four winds. If any man or any nation shall show a desire to trace these roots to their source and obey the law of the Great Peace, they shall be made welcome to take shelter beneath this tree." Many nations took shelter beneath this tree, becoming a part of the first United Nations. Weapons of war were buried deep in the earth.

For many years, the Iroquois Confederacy guarded and protected the Thirteen Colonies from invasion from the north. If it had not been for this protection during the several French and English Wars, it would not have been possible for the United States of America to begin.

Also, white leaders watched the operations of the Iroquois government and learned union and democracy from it. Historians are now beginning to admit what they must have known a long time ago—that the government of the United States is not patterned after something across the ocean, where they believed in the divine right of kings and where the people had no voice, but it is patterned after the government of the People of the Long House, where all people—women as well as men—are represented and control their government.

If any foreign nation insisted upon war to gain its ends, it was always warned three times in open council to obey the law of the Great Peace and settle its disputes by talking them over. If, after the third warning, that nation insisted upon force, it got no other chance. The war Belt was thrown at its feet, and the Five Nations fought it until it was conquered. Their people were not killed or tortured, but were adopted by the Five Nations, assigned lands, and were given the same rights and privileges as other Iroquois. The only freedom they lost was the freedom to wage war.

Because of the Great Law, Kaiianerekowa, the sun shone strong in the hearts of the native peoples of this land. They were a happy people when they lived in North America under the Tree of Peace.

THE MOHAWKS

The Mohawks are a branch of the great Iroquois Confederacy. They are called Ka-nin-ke-a-ka in their own language. The French called them Caniegas. The English called them Mohawks. There were in early days several other Indian nations in and around New York State who were related by blood, culture, and tradition to the Mohawks. The Hurons settled near Georgian Bay and Lake Simcoe. Just north of Lake Erie was an Iroquoian nation called Tionontati or the Tobacco Nation. The Neutral or Neuter Nation lived along the Niagara frontier. In southeastern Virginia lived the Nottoway Indians. Near them lived the Meherrin People. The Erie Indians dwelt south of Lake Erie. East of the Erie Nation in what is now southwestern New York State lived the Wenroe Band. Along the Susquehanna River lived the Susquehannocks or Andastes. In North Carolina two Iroquoian Nations built their towns. They were the Cherokee and the Tuscarora People. In New York State from east to west lived the Mohawks, Oneidas, Onondagas, Cayugas, and Senecas. All of these nations were blood-related and in the distant past had lived as one family west toward the setting sun. Tradition says that they at one time lived in the great Mississippi Valley and were allies of the Wolf or Pawnee Nation but for some unknown reason had migrated east and had become divided.

The Mohawks and other Iroquois tribes were driven from the St. Lawrence Valley by a powerful Algonquin tribe called the Adirondacks. They sought refuge in the land to the south. The Mohawks settled along the banks of the Mohawk River. West of them near Oneida Lake moved the Oneidas. The Onondaga Nation settled near Onondaga Lake. Along Canandaigua Lake the Senecas built their towns and east of them on Lake Cayuga burned the council fire of the Cayuga Nation. Thus central New York came to be the home of the Five Iroquois Nations.

When the Iroquois first came to New York State, it was during a time of great warfare. They built their towns far back in the hills away from the main rivers. They did this because there was less danger from war parties of their enemies. All of these early towns were surrounded by high log stockades for protection against enemy war parties. Later when they had multiplied and had gained strength they moved their villages to the fertile river valleys.

Soon after the Five Nations had settled in New York State, bitter wars broke out between the Senecas and Cayugas on one side and the Mohawks, Oneidas, and Onondagas on the other side. The Mahikans living along the Hudson River, the Hurons north of the Great Lakes, the Susquehannocks of Pennsylvania, and the Eries of the west at the same time sent many war parties against the five disunited Iroquois nations. The Iroquois were in great danger of complete extermination.

About this time two wise men, Deganahwideh, a Huron, and Hiawatha, an Onondaga, sought refuge among the Mohawks. They were adopted by the Mohawks and became sachems of that nation. For five years these two wise men labored to bring about peace between the Five Nations. Finally the Five Iroquois Nations, Mohawks, Oneidas, Onondagas, Cayugas, and Senecas, agreed to bury their differences and join into a League of Peace. Thus came about the Iroquois Confederacy which in time made the Five Nations masters of a territory larger than the whole of Europe. This territory stretched from the Atlantic Ocean to the Mississippi River and from Hudson Bay to North Carolina.

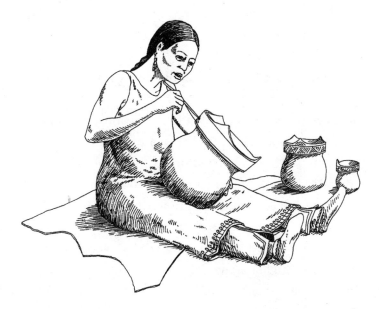

Between 1800 and 1820, bands of Mohawks had reached the western prairies. Some crossed the Rocky Mountains as traders. In 1820 many Mohawks went to live with the Salish and other far western tribes. Some became part of the Salish Nation. Others went down the mouth of the Columbia River in Oregon and north to the Peace River in Alberta. Mohawks settled and married among the Flatheads, Nez Perce, and other western tribes and were responsible for the visit of Father De Smet, the great Jesuit Missionary who, because of their request, went among the far western tribes and worked for their welfare. To this day a band of Mohawks known as Paul's Band, numbering around a hundred and fifty, live on Michel's Reserve in Alberta, Canada. They are descendants of Mohawk voyagers who, in 1804, migrated west to the Athabasca River and settled. Other Mohawks settled among and mingled with the Seneca-Cayuga Indians who had migrated to Ohio and from there were driven by the white men to the far west to what is now Oklahoma.

Because of their great endurance, their skill in hunting and trapping, in handling a canoe, their knowledge of woodcraft and their powerful physical strength, the Mohawks were greatly desired as helpers in the fur trade. Mohawks were in constant demand by all of the great fur companies. They were found in every expedition through and beyond the Great Lakes and to the far north and northwest. Often they would be gone for many years. Even today their love of travel and adventure is well known and their skill as steel workers has carried them to every part of the world.

Perhaps one interested in Iroquois history will wonder what happened to those Mohawks who had been left in the Mohawk Valley, those Mohawks who had not migrated to the Jesuit missions in Canada. Their story is one of tragedy. Because of their ancient treaty made with the Dutch in 1618 and carried on to the English who replaced the Dutch, these Mohawks were in a bad position. Anyone who knows anything of the old Indian character knows that the Indian has never broken a treaty. His word was as good as his bond. Because of this the Mohawks held firmly to the Treaty, the Covenant Chain, that bound them to the English. The settlers did not make matters any better as they were encroaching more and more on Mohawk country in the Mohawk Valley. Though frequently encroached upon and robbed of land, the Mohawks for over three hundred years held fast to this treaty of friendship. In no so-called civilized country can one find a parallel of steadfast faith. When the war between England and the American Colonies broke out, the Mohawks migrated to Canada. They fought fiercely and unwaveringly upon the side of the English because of the peace treaty made many years before. They did not fall upon the American settlements because of any love to fight, to kill or to collect money for scalps from the British. Behind their furious attacks was something more than gain. They were fighting for their homes, their beautiful country along the great river that bears their name. Behind their brave struggle was the hope of regaining their rich corn fields and their great hunting grounds. They knew that if they lost they would become helpless wanderers upon the face of the earth. They expected no mercy from the American settlers and had little faith in the word of the English and for good reason. Though great promises had been made to them by the English in case the English lost, at the close of the war and in the treaty between the two white countries the Iroquois were entirely left out of the agreements. It was with great difficulty that the great Mohawk Captain Joseph Brant, or Thayendanegea, secured lands for his people along the banks of the Grand River. Those Iroquois who had remained in the Mohawk Valley migrated to this new land, now called Six Nation Land, near Ohsweken. Some settled on the Deseronto Reservation, Ontario, Canada.

THE GREAT PEACE

North of the Beautiful Lake, Lake Ontario, on the land of the Huron Nation there was a village. This Huron village was on the Bay of Quinte, where Tyendinaga Mohawk Reservation is today. The Hurons are Iroquoian. They were related by blood to the Five Nations. They had similar language, customs, religion, traditions, and dress.

Living in that Huron village was a virgin woman. This woman was favored by the Creator of All Things. In a vision this woman was told that, though she was married to no man, she was to give birth to a boy child. She was told that she must name this child Deganahwideh. Deganahwideh was to be a great man who was to spread peace and good will among the different nations. He was to plant the Tree of Peace. His life and teachings would someday influence the world. The son was born and the eyes of the Great Spirit ever watched and guarded him from harm. He was given special powers by the Creator.

The boy's grandmother greatly disliked him and often she scolded her daughter for bringing disgrace upon the family. Three times she tried to drown the boy by thrusting him through a hole in the ice of the lake. But the next day the boy was in his lodge by the side of his mother. He seemed well and strong and showed no aftereffect. In a dream the Great Spirit spoke to the old woman, the grandmother. He told her to cease trying to harm the boy, that the boy's mother had born him without having marriage with any man. She was told that the boy was to become an important man.

When Deganahwideh became a man, he was an honest and good man. He had a generous heart. He never killed game for sport but only when he needed food. He shared what he had with the poor and less fortunate of the village. Because of his kindness the birds would light on his shoulders and animals would eat from his hand. He always told what he believed was right. He always spoke against war and talked for peace among all peoples.

One day he bid farewell to his mother and grandmother. In a canoe of white rock (probably birch bark) he paddled across the Beautiful Lake toward the south wind (Little Fawn). He crossed Lake Ontario and paddled up the Oswego River. Crossing Oneida Lake he made a short carry to the Mohawk River. He went eastward down the Mohawk River.

He came to a village of the Flint People, the Mohawks. In those days a stranger never entered an Indian village without an invitation. To do so invited death, as this was during a time of many wars. As was the custom at that time, he made a fire near the village and waited for an invitation to enter. The chiefs sent a scout to ask the stranger, who sat by the fire, to enter their village.

Deganahwideh spoke to the council of the Flint People. He told them of his mission, that he was to speak the works and will of the Creator, the Great Spirit. He told the people that the Great Spirit did not love war. He said that he, Deganahwideh, was sent to establish the Great Peace among the Ongewe-Oweh, the Iroquois, and that nations should no longer kill each other but must smoke the Pipe of Peace and Friendship with each other. "Warfare must cease! To love your brother is better than to hate him. The weapons of war and strife must be buried deep under the earth! To kill is evil!" So said Deganahwideh! The Head Chief of the Flint People agreed with Deganahwideh. He demanded proof, however, that Deganahwideh was the one appointed by the Great Spirit to plant the Tree of Peace and to establish the Great Laws of Friendship. Deganahwideh said that he could prove that he was the messenger of the Great Spirit. Near the village was a high cliff overlooking the lower falls of the Mohawk River. Growing on top of this cliff and overlooking the rough waters of the falls was a huge tree. Deganahwideh said that he would climb the tree and sit on its top branches. The people were to cut down the tree and thus would fall Deganahwideh with it, into the rough waters and sharp rocks below. If he recovered, that was the proof needed. The people agreed, for the cliff was very high, the rocks very sharp, and the waters very rough. They knew that he would surely drown if he was not what he claimed to be. Deganahwideh climbed the tree and it was chopped down. He went beneath the waters and vanished.

The next morning the warriors saw smoke arising from the smoke hole of an empty bark house near the village. There they saw Deganahwideh. He was alive and was smoking while cooking his morning meal. The People of Flint were convinced that Deganahwideh was the one appointed by the Great Spirit to plant the Great Tree of Peace, and that he told the truth.

It was a time of great trouble. The nations of the Iroquois were fighting each other, brothers against brothers. The People of the Flint, (Mohawks), People of the Upright Stone (Oneidas), Hill People (Onondaga), People of the Mucklands (Cayugas), and People of the Great Mountains (Senecas) were continually at war with each other and with outside nations. Because of foolish warfare there were many

people killed. The people mourned the deaths of their loved ones, lost through warfare. People faced starvation because hunters feared to walk alone in the forests, farmers feared to work alone in the gardens. Nowhere was anyone safe. No one knew when the terrible war-cry of the enemy might sound. Fear was constantly in the hearts of the people.

In the country of the Hill People, the Onondagas, near the Onondaga village on Onondaga Lake, there rose the smoke of a lone campfire. It was the fire of Adadarho, the terrible war-chief of the Onondagas. He was feared alike by all nations and even by his own people. This evil man had a body twisted into seven crooks. His long tangled hair was adorned with living serpents. His crooked hand always held a war-club. He was the cause of much hatred and many feuds between the men of the Five Nations. He had great power and was a master of witchcraft. With the use of this wicked power he destroyed many men. Every attempt to destroy Adadarho met with failure. This man was a devourer of raw meat. It is said that he even ate the flesh of humans destroyed in battle.

Though the Onondaga People hated Adadarho, they obeyed him. They feared his sorcery. Finally the Onondagas could endure him no longer. The council asked one called Hayonwatha, who is also called Hiawatha, to clear the mind of the war-chief and to straighten his

crooked body. Hiawatha, who was a man of peace, was determined to make Adadarho cease his evil ways. In canoes the people attempted to cross the lake to Adadarho's camp. When they were in the middle of the lake, Adadarho, shouting in a loud voice, gave his terrible war-cry. The people were frightened and some stood up in the canoes. Their canoes tipped over and many were drowned. Thus the first attempt to meet Adadarho was a failure. Again the people prepared to reason with Adadarho. This time they walked. Adadarho was again ready with his magic power. He caused Akweks, the eagle, to fly close to the heads of the people and to shake his wings, thus loosening many prized eagle feathers. In the rush to secure the feathers, blows were struck and evil feelings were caused. The people forgot their mission. Again the Evil One was stronger.

The people were to try three times before giving up their attempt to win over the war-chief. A certain medicine man told of a vision. He said that Hiawatha alone could not conquer Adadarho. He said that a great man (Deganahwideh) was to come from the north and travel to the east. That great man and Hiawatha together could win over Adadarho. He said that Hiawatha must not remain with the Ononda-gas but must go to the People of the Flint country. The great man from the north lived in a village of the Flint People.

Hiawatha had seven daughters who he greatly loved. The Onondaga people tried to get Hiawatha to go to the Flint country but he
refused to leave his daughters. The people knew that as long as he
had his daughters to keep him that he would never meet Deganahwideh. They decided to kill Hiawatha's daughters through sorcery.
Ohsinoh, a noted shaman was employed to do this. Ohsinoh climbed
a tree near the lodge of one of the daughters and imitating the cry of
a screech owl. He sang a powerful witch song. In three days the
daughter died. He did this in turn to all of the daughters of Hiawatha.
During the night all of the daughters, seven in number, took sick and
died.

The shock and grief of Hiawatha was great. He walked in a daze
but not one of his people came to give him sympathy or comfort. His
mind was shadowed and troubled with his great loss. Those who
belonged to the same clan as Hiawatha's daughters suspected some
kind of mischief. Just before the seventh daughter of Hiawatha took
sick they secretly watched the lodge. They heard the cry of the owl
and heard the witch chant. They followed the singer, Ohsinoh, home

to his own lodge and discovered who he was. When in revenge they lifted their war-clubs to kill him, he gazed at them and their arms were held back by his great power. They could not harm him. Their arrows were held back. The grief of Hiawatha was terrible to behold. When no one punished the shaman he said that he would leave Onondaga. He was determined to become a wanderer in the forest. His anger was so great that the sky shook with thunder. Lightning flashed as, leaving the village, he headed toward the south (Little Fawn).

On the first day he camped on a mountain top. On the second day he camped at the foot of the mountain. On the third day he came to a place where there were many round jointed rushes growing. He cut these into small lengths, thus making beads. He made three strings of these beads. He made a small fire, and sitting near it he said that if he found a person bowed down with grief such as his was that he would mourn with him and try to comfort him. He said that he would lift the clouds of night and darkness from his grieving heart by the use of strings of beads that he had just made. The strings would become words with which he would speak to them. On the fourth day he came to one of the Tully Lakes. He travelled now in an eastern direction (Great Moose). Upon the lake were many ducks.

When they flew upward they lifted the water with them, leaving dry land. (Probably a beaver dam gave out, letting water out and leaving the lake bottom dry. Ducks naturally flew away as they could no longer float.) There were many layers of empty shells of the water snail on the lake bottom. Hiawatha filled a pouch with them. Then the ducks returned and brought the water back with them. (Probably the beavers repaired their dam.) On the fifth day he killed three ducks. On the sixth day he ate some duck meat and went on his way. On the seventh day he went toward the south again (Little Fawn).

He came to an abandoned hut, and there he made a fire and strung some wampum beads of the water snail shells. Sitting near his fire he again said that if he found a person bowed down he grief that he would comfort him by the use of the wampum strings. A chief of a nearby village sent his daughter to invite the stranger to the village. There was a council being held. Hiawatha listened to the speakers, but his opinion was not asked, though he was a chief. Nothing was reported to him. For three days he sat at council listening to the various speakers. On the tenth day he quietly left the village and went his way. The people had not asked his advice and felt that he was not needed.

That day he approached another village. He made a fire outside the village. Over a tripod pole he hung his wampum strings. Sitting near the fire he repeated his words, that if he found a person bowed down with grief such as his was that he would mourn with him and try to comfort him. He said that he would lift the clouds of night and darkness from his grieving heart by the use of the strings of beads that he had just made. The strings would become words with which he would speak to them. A messenger sent by the chief to discover who the stranger was crept near and heard the words of Hiawatha.

He returned to report to his chief. The chief sent the scout to invite Hiawatha to the village. He was asked to sit at council.

On the eighteenth day, a runner came from the south. He told of a great man, Deganahwideh, who had come from the north and was now in a Mohawk village at the lower falls. He told of a vision, that another great man, Hiawatha, was to meet Deganahwideh at Ka-nin-ke-a-ka, Flint Land Village. There shall the two men meet together and establish the Great Peace. The runner was from a nation whose village was at the seashore. So said the messenger from the village on the salt water seashore, who came to tell Hiawatha to journey east. Hiawatha determined to go to the Mohawk country to find the dwelling place of Deganahwideh on the Mohawk River near the lower falls.

The Mohawk River entered the Hudson River, not far from the village and then ran to the salt sea.

The chiefs of the village picked out five skillful scouts to escort Hiawatha. They guided and protected Hiawatha on his journey to the Mohawk Country, to the lodge of Deganahwideh. They watched carefully over his health. It took five days to reach the land of the Flint people. Twenty-three days had passed since Hiawatha had left his own village at Onondaga. On the outside of the Mohawk village they built a fire. It was customary to make a smoke to tell of the approach of visitors so that they might enter the village without endangering their lives. The smoke of Hiawatha's fire floated upward and was seen by the Flint Land People. The Flint People knew the meaning of the smoke signal. A Mohawk messenger invited the party into the village.

Deganahwideh greeted Hiawatha. He saw that he was suffering from some deep grief, that though he was a chief he was not with his own people but was wandering about. Hiawatha told Deganahwideh of his sorrow. At the Mohawk Council Deganahwideh told of the sorrow of Hiawatha. He mourned with Hiawatha. He tried to comfort him in his great loss. He sought to take away the clouds from the heart of the chief so that he could see more clearly. Deganahwideh strung eight more strands of wampum. There were eight parts of Deganahwideh's address to console Hiawatha. His words were in thirteen strings of wampum, bound in four bunches.

Deganahwideh took one bunch from the pole. Holding it and the bunches, one by one, he handed them to Hiawatha after each part of his address. The words that he spoke to Hiawatha were eight of the thirteen condolences. Deganahwideh said that in the future wampum strings would be held in the hand to remind the speaker of each part of his talk and when each address is finished, a string would be given to the mourning chief on the opposite side of the fire. The bereaved chief will hold them and then hand them back, one by one, as he gives a reply. After the eight ceremonial addresses had been made by the great Mohawk chief, the mind of Hiawatha was made clear.

Once more he saw things clearly. Once more the sun shone in his heart. The Mohawk Chief then said that because Hiawatha's mind was now strong and clear, that he was capable of judging and could now help him make the laws for the Great Peace whose purpose would be to do away war, death, and robbery between brothers and bring peace, quietness, and brotherhood among mankind.

They now composed their Peace Song. It would, if sung without any error, straighten the wicked mind of Adadarho. The emblem of the

Confederate chiefs are deer antlers which should be worn by them at council. The two men then told the Mohawk Council of their plan for a Confederation of peace and the building of a Long House of brotherhood and peace. The Chiefs were told that they must be very virtuous, patient men, that they should wear deer antlers as an emblem of their position.

Before they could proceed with their plans, it was necessary to know the opinion of the Mohawk Council. The plan was talked about in the council. The Mohawk speaker said that they, the Mohawks, would firmly grasp the Tree of Peace and would work hard for brotherhood between nations. Their hearts were happy at the thought of ceasing warfare.

Scouts were sent to the People of the Upright Stone, the Oneidas, to see what they thought of the plan for everlasting peace. The plan was talked about at the council of the Oneidas. After considering the plan for one year, Quiver Bearer, head chief of the Oneidas, said that the People of the Upright Stone would join the Confederation. Two messengers were sent toward the setting sun. They carried wampum strings and an invitation to join the Confederation. They arrived in the country of the People of the Muckland or the Great Pipe People, the Cayugas. They built their fire as was the custom and recited their message. One year from that date the Cayugas sent back word to the Mohawk Council that they had considered the plan, had agreed with Deganahwideh, and would hold fast to the Tree of Peace.

A runner was sent to the People of the Great Hill, the Senecas. They lived far toward the setting sun, toward the west. The Senecas were divided in their opinion. One large band lived west of the Genesee River. They were friends of the Erie Nation who were against the League. The band who lived near the Great Mountains, near Canandaigua Lake, were for the League.

Messengers built their smoke fires near both bands and they were both invited to join the Confederacy. The People of the Great Hill were not united very strongly at that time. There had been trouble between their war-chiefs. They asked the messengers of Deganahwideh to return the next year and they would have an answer by that time.

Both councils finally listened and considered the peace proposals. They finally agreed with Deganahwideh and after a year, they sent messengers to the Mohawk Council to say that they had agreed to enter the Confederacy, that they would grasp the Tree of Peace.

The Onondaga Nation, the People of the Hills, had been approached before. They wanted to join the peace league but had hesitated to agree openly because of their great fear of Adadarho. When a messenger approached them, however, they agreed to grasp the Tree of Peace. At the great council of the Mohawks, when all of the people were present, Deganahwideh and Hiawatha reported all that had been done during the five successive years. Deganahwideh said that he had obtained the consent of the Five Nations, the Mohawks, Oneidas, Onondagas, Senecas, and Cayugas, to form a peace compact for the union of the Nations. He said that these Five Nations had agreed to bury their differences and establish a great peace league whose aim was to eventually take in all of the tribes; its object, to do away with war.

Deganahwideh then said that they must find out where the fire of Adadarho burned, that it was he who was the cause of much trouble between the nations of men. "We must seek him out and cure his crooked mind." said the Great Chief.

The Mohawk speaker for the council agreed and confirmed all that Deganahwideh and said. Deganahwideh then asked for two scouts (Wolves) who would offer to seek out the smoke of Adadarho. Two men quickly offered to become scouts. The head man asked them if they had the ability of the animals and birds of the forests, for such they must have if they were clever enough to approach the terrible warrior and not be caught. The two volunteers said that they would be as clever as herons and cranes. After looking them over, the head man said that they would not do because the heron and the crane would stop at the first river or lake for frogs and fish.

Again the head man asked for two scouts who would offer to seek out the smoke of Adadarho. Two men quickly offered to become scouts. The head man asked them if they had the ability of the animals and birds of the forests, for such they must have if they were clever enough to approach the terrible warrior and not be caught. The two volunteers said that they would be as clever as hummingbirds and would fly very swiftly. After looking them over, the head man said that they would not do because the hummingbird is always hungry and is always looking for flowers.

Again the head man asked for two scouts who would offer to seek out the smoke of Adadarho. Two men quickly offered to become scouts. The head man asked them if they had the ability of the animals and birds of the forests, for such they must have if they were clever enough to approach the terrible warrior and not be caught. The two volunteers said that they would be as clever as the white crane. After looking them over, the head man said that they would not do because the white crane is very wild and easily frightened, that they would fly in terror when the clouds moved and would forget their mission.

Again the head man asked for two scouts who would offer to seek out the smoke of Adadarho. Two more men asked to be allowed to seek out Adadarho's fire. They said that they would be like crows and would fly straight to the lodge of the terrible war-chief. The Head man said that they would not do, as crows are too noisy, that they talk too loudly, boast, and are full of mischief. Adadarho would hear them long before they found his fire.

Again the head man asked for two scouts who would offer to seek out the smoke of Adadarho. Finally two skilled warriors stepped forward and offered to serve as scouts. They said that they were strong as the deer and bear and had their power.

These two were chosen to seek the smoke of the war-chief. The head man, the speaker for the council, reported that the two scouts were ready for their trial. The two scouts travelled through the forest on their mission. They traveled toward the south wind, the "Little Fawn."

Deganahwideh spoke to the Mohawk Council. "I and my younger brother, Hiawatha, stand before you. We now place before you the laws by which to frame the Great Peace," said Deganahwideh. The great leader said, "The symbol of our Peace League will be the Tree of Peace, the white pine. Watching over the welfare of our people and perched upon the Tree of Peace will be the eagle, guardian bird of our people. His far-seeing eyes will warn us of the approach of enemies.

Under the Tree of Peace we must bury all the weapons of war and bloodshed. Men of the Five Nations must unite and always act as one heart, one mind, and one soul. They must forever spread good will and brotherhood among all nations, always remembering that the main object of the Confederacy is to make possible . . . peace, prosperity, power, and equality for all!

"The emblems of the leaders of the Confederacy shall be the antlers of the deer. The chieftainship titles of the clans of the Five Nations (heron, eel, deer, bear, wolf, turtle, snipe, beaver, eagle) shall be placed in the hands of certain women and the titles or names of these chiefs shall be held in the families of the mothers forever."

Deganahwideh then recited all the laws of the Confederacy, recording each with a string of wampum. Hiawatha confirmed all that

Deganahwideh said. Deganahwideh then sang the song that was to be used in the ceremony when a leader received his chieftainship title. Chiefs were to have the power but they must abide by the will of the people. A chief must think of the welfare of his people above all things. His own interests must always come last. The Head Man told the chief and the people that they must never forget the Great Spirit, that they must always ask his aid and power to help them be good leaders. The chiefs must firmly grasp the Tree of Peace. They must never forget the purpose for which the League was formed.

The scouts then returned to the Mohawk Council. They reported to the leaders and to Deganahwideh. The scouts reported that they had discovered the fire of Adadarho at great danger to themselves. They said that the hair of the warrior resembled live snakes, that when Adadarho was angry the snake hair seemed to hiss and spit. They reported that the body of the terrible war-chief was deformed, that it had seven crooks in it. The scouts said that he always held a war-club knotted in his hands, which are like the claws of a wild animal. "He is a cannibal," they said.

Deganahwideh then walked back and forth before the Long House. He sang the Hymn of Peace and other sacred songs. He taught the people the Hymn of Peace. Many people came and learned the Peace Hymn. They were made strong with the power of the songs. The Hymn of Peace had great power.

When the grass was knee high, when the season was midsummer, Deganahwideh called all of the People of Flint together, men, women, children. He chose one man to go ahead. This man was to approach Adadarho and sing the Hymn of Peace before his lodge. They, the Mohawk People, travelled toward the west wind, toward the "Great Panther." The singer led the company through the forests singing the Peace Songs as he went. The Mohawks followed the singer. There were many tracks through the forests made by the many people. Many old villages and camping places were passed as they went toward the Onondaga country. The names of the villages were lifted to give to the Clan Name Holders. Now they were in the territory of the People of the Upright Stone, the Oneidas. There they met the great Oneida Chief, Quiver Bearer with his chiefs and his people. All of the two nations, the Mohawks and Oneidas, marched on toward the country of the Hill People, the Onondaga, the singer of the Peace Songs going ahead. As the Mohawks and Oneidas walked together through the forests, they met the Great Pipe People, the Cayuga, and also the People of the Great Mountain, the Senecas. They greeted each other in friendship and the great throng headed toward the country of the People of the Hills. Together the trails of all four nations, Mohawks, Oneidas, Cayugas, and Senecas, marched through the forests toward the Onondaga settlements.

When the country of the Onondagas was reached, the people halted their march. They kindled a fire as was customary. The chiefs of the Onondagas welcomed them. A great multitude marched to the fireside of Adadarho. The singer of the Hymn of Peace led the throng.

The chiefs and people of the Mohawks, Oneidas, Onondagas, Cayugas, and Senecas all walked toward the lodge of the terrible warrior. The people gathered before the lodge of Adadarho. The singer walked before the lodge of the terrible warrior. He tried to cure the sick mind of the warrior by singing the Peace Hymn. It was necessary to sing the Peace Hymn without error if it was to work any power on the mind of the terrible warrior. The singer hesitated and made an error in the song. Another singer was appointed but he also made an error in the song. Then Deganahwideh walked before the door of the house of Adadarho. He sang the song without any error. Adadarho heard the song and his power was broken. His war-club dropped from his gnarled hands. When he had finished his song, Deganahwideh walked toward Adadarho and rubbed his body to give it strength and life. Because of the power of Deganahwideh and of the Peace Hymn, the body of Adadarho was made straight. His mind was made healthy. His heart became as a pine tree, clean and good. After the mind and body of Adadarho had become healed, Deganahwideh spoke to the gathering of the nations. He said that the greatest obstacle in the way of a lasting peace had been removed, that the mind of Adadarho had been purified and his body and soul cleansed of all evil. "Now that that is done, we may devote ourselves to establishing the Great Peace," said the Great Man.

Deganahwideh said, "In every nation there are wise and pure men. These men should be appointed to become chiefs of their people. They will be advisors of their people and will make any new laws that will be needed. They are to be selected by the Clan Mothers, but must have the good will of the entire Clan. When these chiefs are selected, they will be crowned with deer antlers, emblems of friendship," said Deganahwideh.

The Clan Mothers of the People of Flint, the Mohawks, brought forward nine chiefs and one war-chief. They, the chiefs, were of the clans Bear, Wolf, and Turtle.

The Clan Mothers of the People of the Upright Stone, the Oneidas, brought forward nine chiefs and one war-chief. They, the chiefs, were of the clans Bear, Wolf, and Turtle.

The Clan Mothers of the People of the Hills, the Onondagas, brought forward fourteen chiefs and one war-chief. They were of the clans Turtle, Snipe, Bear, Deer, Wolf, and Ball.

The Clan Mothers of the People of the Great Pipe or the People of the Mucklands, the Cayuga, brought forward ten chiefs and one war-chief. They were of the clans Heron, Deer, Turtle, Bear, and Snipe.

The Clan Mothers of the People of the Great Hill, the Senecas, brought forward eight chiefs and one war-chief. They were of the clans Bear, Snipe, Turtle, Wolf, and Eagle.

Deganahwideh then said to the chiefs, "I place upon your heads deer antlers as emblems of your power. Your old names are taken away and new names, which have more power, are given to you. Your patience must be very great, seven thumbs thick. You must walk and work in unity. Never think of your own interests, but work to benefit the people and those yet unborn. All of your power comes from the Great Peace and you must pledge yourselves to it. Deganahwideh repeated all of the laws he and Hiawatha had created for the building of the Great Peace. The fifty chiefs of the Mohawks, Oneidas, Onondagas, Cayugas, and Senecas each gave to Deganahwideh a string of lake-shell wampum as a pledge of truth and loyalty to the Laws of the Great Peace.

Deganahwideh made the Onondagas the Firekeepers and the Capital of the Confederacy. Adadarho was made the Firekeeper of the sacred fire burning at Onondaga. He was made the chief speaker at the Confederate Council.

Deganahwideh said that a chief must always speak the truth. A chief, must be kind, considerate, generous, and must always consider the welfare of his people. He must give freely of what he owns to his people, especially the poor and less fortunate. He must always be ready to help those of his people who are in want or need. His aid must be given willingly and he must receive no pay or reward for his services. He must even be willing to give away his own personal belongings, even skins and meat, if it will better his people by doing so. A chief must never forget the Creator of Mankind. He must even ask the Great Spirit for help and assistance. He must always remember the Laws of the Great Peace. They must come before every other thought. The chiefs of the Five Nations must council and work together. They must work in unity and not try to do things separately, less their nation become divided. Any great move, step, or act must have the consent of all of the Five Nations. A chief must be very wise, very patient. He must never let his temper get the best of him, less he not

39

be able to cast good judgement. His skin must be seven thumbs thick. Always must he remember that the Great Confederacy was organized for peace. Peace and friendship among all people was the main aim of the Great Law.

The Mohawks, Oneidas, Onondagas, Cayugas, and Senecas are as one nation or people. They are bound together. As one people they must work together. Only in unity will there be strength. The Head Men must always remember that other nations are to be invited to take shelter beneath the Tree of Long Leaves. The eagle on top of the tree will guard and watch all peoples who wish to rest under the tree. To the four corners of the world, North (Bear), West (Panther), East (Moose), and South (Fawn), the chiefs of the Confederacy are to send messengers inviting all to take shelter beneath the Great Tree of Peace, to join the Confederacy. The war-clubs and other weapons of war are to be buried by all who accept the Great Peace.

Deganahwideh took a string of wampum and held it before the multitude saying, "It is provided thus: I and the Confederate Lords have now planted a tree of Great Peace, Kayaneregowah, in your settlement, Adadarho, Onondagas the Firekeepers. This Tree of Great Peace, I hereby name Jonerahdesegowah. Under the shade of the Tree of Great Peace, we spread this Jonodakenrahgowah, the belt of white wampum. On it we have prepared for you, Adadarho, and your cousin Lords, seats. We now put you and your cousin Lords on the seats of prepared wampums spread under the shades of the spreading branches of the Tree of Great Peace, to keep and watch the Confederate Council Fire; and all the business of the Confederate Nation will be transacted at this place, before you, Adadarho, and your cousin Lords, Jarasentshenh."

Deganahwideh took a second wampum belt and held it before the multitude saying, "It is provided thus: A root has grown out of this Tree of Great Peace; one to the north, one to the south, one to the east, and another to the west. The names of these roots are Ohdehrakenrahgowah, meaning Big White Root, and the nature of it is peace and charity. If any nation or individual outside of the Confederacy shall adopt the Laws of the Great Peace, Kayanerenhgowah, when they are made known to him or them by the Lords of the Five

Confederate Nations, trace the roots to the Tree of Great Peace, discipline their minds and spirits to obey, honor the wishes of the Imperial Council Fire of the Confederacy, they are welcome to take shelter under its spreading branches. We now place an Eagle on the top of the Tree of Great Peace; it can be seen a great distance, and if there is anything dangerous to the lives of the Confederate Nations, that which would be approaching, the bird shall warn them at once."

Deganahwideh took a third string of wampum and held it before the multitude saying, "It is provided thus: To you, Adadarho, and your cousin Lords, fourteen of you altogether, this shall be your duty. You shall keep the Confederate Council Fire clean all around, you shall allow no dust or dirt to be seen around the Council Fire. I therefore lay a seagull wing, Shaweyesehgowah Onerahontshah, near you. Take this wing and sweep the dust and dirt away from the Council Fire. If you see any crawling creature approaching the Confederate Council Fire, I lay a stick by you with which you are to pitch the crawling creature from the Council Fire, and your cousin Lords will act with you at all times. Dust, dirt, and crawling creatures signify a matter or proposition brought before the Council which would be injurious to the Confederate Nation. If you fail to reject it alone, you shall call the rest of your Confederate Lords to your aid."

Deganahwideh, one by one, took eighty-two wampum strings and belts, one for each of the laws of the Great Peace, and held them before the multitude, at the same time telling the people what each string or belt signified. Thus was formed the Great Confederation of the Five Nations in the days before the arrival of white-faced invaders from the Big Salt Water to the east.

THE ARRIVAL OF THE EUROPEANS

A cloud of darkness was to come to the Haudenosaunee, the People of the Long House. From across the ocean came the French and the English. These two invaders desired furs and eventually the lands of the Five Nations. Both gave the Iroquois guns, tomahawks, and liquor for beaver skins. Though these two held out one hand in pretended friendship, their other hand held a rattlesnake whose bite was poison and death.

The first contact that the white man had with the Iroquois was in 1535 when Jacques Cartier made his exploration of the St. Lawrence River in search of a passage to India and China. Everywhere Cartier found friendly natives and by them he was received in the kindest manner. At the Rock of Quebec he found an Iroquois Village called Stadacona. On the Isle of Montreal he visited another Iroquois town called Hochelaga. There he was royally entertained by a Mohawk chief. When Cartier returned to France he took with him as a prisoner this Mohawk chief who had treated him with such hospitality and kindness.

Both the French and English, being jealous of the fur trade and desiring the whole of it, talked the various Indian Nations near their settlements into making war against their rivals and those Indians who brought furs to their rivals.

In 1609 Samuel de Champlain and two other Frenchmen, accompanying a war party of Ottawa and Huron Indians, met a party of Mohawks near a spot where Fort Ticonderoga now stands. The two parties agreed to fight on the following day. The bows and arrows of the Mohawks were no match for the guns of the Frenchmen. Three of the Mohawk chiefs fell at the first fire. It was the first time that the Iroquois had ever heard the thundering roar of a gun, as well as the appearance of a strange people with white skins and hairy faces, confused them and they fled to the forest. Though this was a victory for the Frenchmen, it caused in the hearts of the Iroquois a deadly hated for the French. This hatred lasted a century and a half and in the end it caused the downfall of the French colonies in the new world.

In 1615, Champlain, with a war party of Hurons and Algonquins, again entered the Iroquois country. Their plan was to invade the entire Iroquois country and to exterminate them. Near Nichols Pond the party discovered a strongly fortified village of Oneidas. They were unsuccessful in destroying this village and their expedition was a failure. Champlain was wounded and had to be carried home in a basket. This battle showed the Iroquois that the white man with his gun could be conquered. It also increased the hatred that the Iroquois had for the French.

In 1609 Henry Hudson sailed up the Hudson River. There he came in contact with Mahikans and other friendly Indian tribes. The Dutch, five years later, built a trading post near where Albany now stands. In 1618 the Dutch made a treaty with the Iroquois. This "Chain of Friendship" between the Dutch and the Mohawks was later taken over by the English and has lasted to the present day. From the Dutch, the Mohawks and other Iroquois secured firearms and with these brought terror to the hearts of the French and those Indians who were allies of them. Up until twenty-four years after Champlain had killed the three Mohawk chiefs, the Iroquois had not tried to kill any Frenchmen though many Iroquois had been slain by the French. Patiently they had waited to avenge their slain brothers. Now that they had secured firearms, they felt strong enough to revenge the insults of Champlain and his people. They turned on the French and their allies and one by one they exterminated those nations who had aided the French. The Algonquins from Lake Nippissing to Saguenay, the Hurons, the Nipissings, the Ottawa, the Adirondacks, the Tiontati, the Susquehannocks, the Miamis, the Illinois, the Delawares, and others who had aided the French or who had refused to cease warfare and to grasp the Tree of Peace of the Iroquois Confederacy were exterminated and their remnants adopted into the ranks of the Five Nations.

The French colonies depended upon the fur trade for their existence. The war parties of the Iroquois practically put an end to all French fur trade. The Iroquois invaded the Island of Montreal and had wiped out every Frenchman in the entire colony who had not secured protection in the fort at the time.

During the wars in Europe between the French and the English, these two nations who had colonies in America spared no effort to get the different Indian nations in America to fight against their rivals in the New World. Both the French and the English desired the fur trade of the Iroquois and other Indian nations. Both the French and the English cast greedy eyes on the lands of the Iroquois. Both claimed the Iroquois country as their own. The Iroquois never acknowledged either the French or the English as having any claim over them or their country. The English governor encouraged the Five Nations to attack the French and their Indian allies. The French likewise encouraged the Hurons, Eries, and other Indian nations to attack the English and the Iroquois. The unfortunate Iroquois whose Confederacy had been formed to bring about peace tried in vain to get the French and the English to cease warfare and invited them to take shelter under the Tree of Peace. Their efforts were in vain. The Five Nations living between these two rival white colonies realized that they were being used as tools, and during all of the wars between the French and the English they, the Iroquois, were the main ones to suffer. Because of the wars between the white men they, the Five Nation Iroquois, as a people, were to dwindle to less than half of their original number. Yet they stuck to their treaty with the English, and their vain attempt at peace, continuing to spread terror among the French until that people were defeated.

France realized that if she were to keep her colonies in the New World she must somehow get the Iroquois away from British influence. Subsequent to the Treaty of 1666 France took advantage of the period of peace. Jesuit missionaries were sent among the Mohawks and other Iroquois Nations. In 1667 three Jesuit missionaries,

Jacques Fremin, Jean Pierron, and Jacques Bruyas, visited the Mohawks in the Mohawk River Valley. They preached at the Mohawk Village Kahnawake. Julien Garnier, Pierre Milet, and Etienne de Carheil preached in other Iroquois villages. Up until this time all Jesuit missionaries among the Iroquois had met with failure and sometimes death. By 1668 all of the Five Nations had Jesuit missionaries. The Jesuits encouraged the Iroquois to leave their homelands and establish communities just outside of Montreal.

Most of the Iroquois sided with the English. They easily defeated the French and their Indian allies.

The French tried to wean the Iroquois away from their friendship with the English. Black Robes, the Jesuits from Canada, went among the Iroquois and especially among the Mohawks. They told them about Christianity and tried to get them to migrate to Canada. Many listened to the Black Robes. Their footsteps headed north.

They founded a new settlement on the St. Lawrence River. This they named Kahnawake. Many of the Iroquois left their villages and went to live at Kahnawake. On the other side of the river across from Kahnawake was the French town of Montreal. Most of the Indians who settled at Kahnawake were Mohawks but there were also Oneidas, Onondagas, Cayugas, and Senecas.

More wars among the white men followed. Both the English and the French urged the Indian people who lived near them to fight what they then called, "Our common enemy." Forgotten were the words of the two wise prophets, Deganahwideh and Hiawatha. Now we find Iroquois from Kahnawake fighting against Iroquois who lived to the south of them, blood against blood, clan against clan, Mohawk against Mohawk. The result was that many were killed.

After the war, the Kahnawakes were moved many times but still across the St. Lawrence River loomed the large town of Montreal.

Traders from Montreal would cross the river and visit the Indian town. With them they brought along their vice, alcohol. This made the Mohawks crazy and the Evil Spirit possessed them. In vain the Black Robes tried to stem the evil influence from across the river. Many times they moved the Indian people to get away from this evil.

Strange diseases such as smallpox, measles, and whooping cough began to appear among the Indian people. Many were sick and many died. The hearts of those who were left were filled with a dark cloud. It was the dark cloud of fear and sorrow. Their old men said that they must get away from this evil from across the river. Their Jesuit Fathers agreed with them. Many of them packed their goods on their backs and headed up the St. Lawrence River.

Far up the St. Lawrence River they found a beautiful spot. Many smaller rivers entered the St. Lawrence River near this place. The soil was fertile. There was good hunting and fishing. But above all they were alone without any harm from outside influence. They erected a church on a beautiful point of land that extended into the river. Around their church they built their cabins.

They called their new home, Akwesasne, or the Place Where the Partridge Drums.

CHRISTIAN CONVERSIONS

In 1667 an Oneida named Tonsohoten, and five others were baptized and were persuaded to settle at Laprarie on the St. Lawrence River across from Montreal. Following this, many converts began to leave their villages along the Mohawk River. At Laprarie the Indian Mission of St. Francis Xavier was founded. By 1670 twenty Indian families had settled there. Father Philippi Pierson was sent as an assistant. In 1671 Father Jacques Fremin took his place. The migrant Iroquois were placed under the guardianship of the Jesuit Society. The Jesuits, anxious for the welfare of their converts, tried to stem the liquor traffic which the officials of the West India Company encouraged among the Mohawks and other Indians. Their reason for encouraging strong drink was to make it easier to swindle the Indians out of their furs and other products. Fremin, especially, tried to check this curse which was draining the life blood of the Iroquois. Meanwhile more and more Iroquois migrated to Canada. In less than seven years there were more Mohawk converts at Laprarie than in their own country along the Mohawk River. The Mohawks were not the only Indians who settled at Laprarie. According to the old Jesuit records there was at one time over twenty two Indian nations represented at Laprarie. Of these the Mohawks were the majority. The Onondagas and Hurons were next.

Through a quarrel over chiefs, the Hurons separated themselves from the others and started a new mission beyond the river. This mission was founded by the Sulpicians in 1676 at the foot of Mount Royal. It was made up of Iroquois and Algonquin converts. When the Huron converts from Laprarie joined them, it grew rapidly. In twenty years another division was made. Two hundred Indians went to live at Sault au Recollet. In 1704 a second division took place. The Iroquois remained at Mount Royal and Sault au Recollet, while the Algonquins went to Baied Urfe. A number of Nipissings migrated to Isle Aux Tourtes at the foot of Two Mountains. In 1721 the Sulpicians brought these tribes together and formed a large mission at Oka.

Gandeakteua, an Erie woman and wife of Tonsohoten, one of the first converts, was a famous and influential woman of this period of Iroquois extraction. It is said that she was a very pious person and model of virtue. Her cabin was a home to all and by her influence many were converted. In 1671 it was she who helped Father Fremin and Father Pierson found the Sodality of the Holy Family, an organization still flourishing after two hundred years. It is said that she had the reputation of a saint.

A famous Mohawk warrior of this period was Athasta or Kryn, the Great Mohawk. It was he who, during August 1669, led the Mohawks against the Mahikans and defeated them. While visiting Laprarie he became converted. Because of his influence a band of forty men, women, and children under Father Boniface left the Mohawk River and settled at Laprarie.

Meanwhile liquor from the traders across the river was having its bad effect on the Mohawks of Laprarie in spite of all the missionaries could do. Because of this Father Fremin and the Mohawks bid farewell to Laprarie and moved to the foot of the Rapids. The new mission was called Kahnawake or St. Xavier of the Sault. In 1673 the Hurons for the same reason moved to Lorette.

In 1676 a group of Huron visited the Kahnawake community. As a pledge of goodwill and friendship they left a wampum belt with the Mohawks. This belt means that the Kahnawake Mohawks must make a strong fight against the evil, liquor, which was the cause of the ruin of both the Huron and Kahnawake Missions. It also means that they should be good Christians. This belt now rests in the Kahnawake Mission on the Kahnawake Reservation, Quebec, Canada. (Update: this belt was stolen within the last the last two decades.)

Another famous woman of this period was Kateri Tekakwitha who was born in 1656. She was eleven years old when Fathers Fremin, Bruyas, and Pierron visited her village of Kahnawake on the Mohawk River. In 1675 she was baptized. In 1677 she moved to Laprarie. Her entire life was one of purity and holiness and her remains in the Kahnawake Church have at various times worked many cures and miracles for those who have had faith.

In 1678 the dread white man's disease, small pox, struck Kahnawake and many died. On August 20, 1683, another catastrophe hit the new settlement. Their church caved in. But the main trouble of the convert Iroquois was the constant quarrels and wars between the French and the English who were unwilling to leave the Indians out of their disputes. Not only the French of Canada but the English along the Hudson valued the fur trade. Neither side had any scruples over using the Iroquois when it suited their purpose. The colonial fur traders, both French and English, generally despised the Indians and treated them little better than the animals of the forest. Their chief aim and use of the Indian was of commercial value only, to gather pelts or scalps, a custom that they introduced to many Indian tribes. The Indians were often cheated out of their furs. In many instances they were fed liquor until they lost their reason, were slain, and their furs stolen. It was against these unscrupulous traders that the missionaries had their greatest trouble.

Col. Dongan, Governor of New York, made many efforts to alienate the Christian Iroquois from the French. He spread word among the Five Nations of New York State that the new French Governor, De Denonville, was planning to exterminate them. In 1686, De Denonville asked the Onondaga missionaries to have a delegation of Iroquois chiefs meet him in council. Forty chiefs, laden with gifts, were seized by orders of the French governor, were bound and taken to Quebec where they were condemned to work as slaves in Europe. This act of treachery hurt all missions and endangered the lives of all missionaries working among the Iroquois. In anger they, the Iroquois, returned to their old homes along the Mohawk.

In 1690, to again get away from the evil influence across the river, the convert Mohawks moved their village to a new site farther west. They called it Kahnawakon.

FRENCH AND ENGLISH WARS

Meanwhile the French and English were again at war. Behind the Iroquois who had remained at home in their home territory were the English colonial officials urging the Iroquois on to attack the French. Even when the Five Nations were tired of war, the colonial officials sent three deputies to persuade them not to make peace or to consent to an armistice but to continue to fight the French and their Indian allies. In 1691 Major Peter Schuyler traveled Lake Champlain and attacked Fort Laprarie. He was defeated by the Mohawks of Kanawakon who came to the rescue of the French army. Frontenac, the French Governor, tried very hard to get the Christian Mohawks to kill those Mohawks who had accompanied Schuyler.

The Mohawk Indians both along the St. Lawrence River and along the Mohawk River desired peace and were willing to keep peace and to trade with both the French and the English. They claimed independence of both. The English tried to get the Mohawks from along the Mohawk River to fight against their brothers who had their village on the banks of the St. Lawrence River. The French tried to get the St. Lawrence Mohawks to fight against their brothers living along the Mohawk River. The white men were foolish to hope that they could get the Mohawks to fight against their own countrymen.

In 1696 there was a third transfer of the Mission of St. Francis Xavier to the new Indian village of Kanawake opposite Devils Island.

In 1716 a few Mohawks migrated to a new village site, Kahnawake, which was three miles west of La Susanne along the riverfront on land that had been added to the original grant of 1680. The abandoned village from which they had moved was ever afterward called Kanatakwenke or "Where the Village was Taken From."

Father Huc Francois Nou, who was welcomed at Kahnawake in 1735 wrote, "Generally speaking, you could find nowhere finer looking men. They are better built than the French, while side by side with the Iroquois, other Indians seemed dwarfed."

Paul Ragueneau, in the *Relation of 1650,* wrote, "It is customary with these people that when refugees seek cover among strangers, their hosts distribute them among the different cabins. They give them not only lodging but food as well." Again he writes, "I have often seen this hospitality practiced among the Hurons, when seven or eight hundred fugitives would find, from the moment they arrived, benevolent entertainers who stretched out their arms to them and joyfully came to their assistance."

At the same period the English Governor, Hon. Cadwallader Colden, wrote of the Five Nations of New York State, "None of the greatest Roman heroes have discovered greater love for their country or a greater contempt of death than these people have done, when liberty came in competition. I think our Indians have outdone the Romans in this particular; some of the greatest of those have we known murdered themselves to avoid shame and torments; but our Indians have refused to die meanly, or with little pain, when they thought their country's honour would be at stake by it; but have given their bodies, willingly, to the most cruel torments of their enemies, to shew, as they said, that the Five Nations consisted of men, whose courage and resolution could not be shaken."

It had been the plan of both the French and the English to secure lands of the Indians and to weaken the tribes by urging them to fight against themselves. Because of this European practice most of the Indian tribes were considerably reduced.

The chief aim of the French Government was to bring all of the Iroquois into closer relations to the French. This would reduce the number of those who might help the English. The Indians would also be an advantage to the French colony because in time of war the Iroquois would be the watch dogs of the French and would form a barrier which would protect Montreal against all raids by the English. Duesque and other French Governors did not hesitate to encourage and even demand that the Kahnawake Mohawks should attack those Mohawks who had refused to move to Kahnawake near the French settlement.

In 1749 Francis Picquet, a Sulpitian, tried to draw the Iroquois away from the English. He formed a settlement, a missionary station, and built a fort near the mouth of the Oswegatchie River. Indian Point in Lisbon about three miles below Ogdensburg was the site of this Oswegatchie Indian Village. In 1806 New York State took over the lands of these Indians and forced them to move away. The remnants of the Oswegatchie went to live among the St. Regis and Onondaga Indians.

In 1759 a band of Mohawks led by Father Gordan, Superior at Kahnawake, left Kahnawake and travelling up the St. Lawrence River they formed a new Mohawk settlement along its banks, at the confluence of the St. Regis, Racquette, and Grasse Rivers. This village was placed under the patronage of St. John Francis Regis, a Jesuit of the eighteenth century who had done great work among the poor of France. The Kahnawake Mohawks as a pledge of good will to their departing brothers made them a gift of some precious relics among which was the skull and some of the bones of their great Mohawk sister, Kateri Tekakwitha, the Lily of the Mohawks.

These relics were placed in the new church at St. Regis and were held in great veneration by the St. Regis Mohawks. When the old church burned down, the sacred relics were destroyed. The St. Regis settlement has also been called Akwesasne, the Place Where the Partridge Drums.

After the Treaty of 1763, many of the Mohawks from Kahnawake moved to the Ohio Valley and formed a Mohawk Colony near Sandusky and Scioto. They numbered around two hundred at the outbreak of the Revolutionary War.

THE CODE OF HANDSOME LAKE

To give the full life of Handsome Lake and all of the lessons that he taught would take considerable space. Out of the 130 sections of the Handsome Lake Religion, I will describe in brief his main teachings and their effect upon the present day Iroquois.

This story is about the People of the Great Mountain, Seneca Nation. Many winters in the past, in 1735 at the Seneca town of Conawagus on the Genesee River there was born an Indian boy who was later to become one of the greatest Indian prophets and teachers of recent historical date. This Seneca was later given the office of Chief of the Turtle Clan, with the title of Kaniatario or Handsome Lake.

At that time the white settlers took over the beautiful lands of the Seneca Nation along the Genesee River. There was unhappiness in the hearts of the Senecas because of the loss of their beautiful river. The Senecas packed their belongs on their backs and set out toward the setting sun. Some of them settled on a new reservation near the Allegheny Mountains. They built a town on the Allegheny River.

The Senecas often paddled their canoes down the Allegheny River to a fur trading town, Pittsburg. There they would trade furs and skins for rum. On the way home they lashed their canoes together. Those who were intoxicated took the inside canoes. Because of the danger of being drowned they had to return home in this manner. The people would flee when the warriors returned. They would be drunk beyond reason as they kicked down doors and trampled fires. Destruction and death always followed the return of the warriors from the trading town down the river.

Handsome Lake became very ill from too much use of alcohol. While drunk he did many evil things. He even sang the sacred songs while under the influence of liquor. For four years he was so ill that he could not stand but was confined to his bed. Many times during the four years he thought that he would die. During these times he thought much of the things that the Great Spirit had created. He saw and felt the warm rays of the sun. At night he admired the beauty of

the moon and the shining stars. He listened to the songs of the birds. He thanked the Creator for these things and asked to get well again.

One morning his daughter and her husband were shelling beans outside of the house. They heard a sound and looking up they saw their father, Handsome Lake, slowly walk out of the door. He staggered and fell to the earth. There he died. They quickly summoned his clan relatives. They dressed him in his ceremonial clothes for burial. His relatives came in silence; they sat around the dead chief's body. From the time of dew until high noon they sat watching the dead chief. At high noon Handsome Lake sat up! When he spoke he said, "I have seen wonderful things."

He said, "A voice called me out of the cabin. I arose and walked out. Three wonderful appearing men stood before me. In one hand they held bows and arrows and in the other hand they held bunches of huckleberries of every color. The three men said, 'Eat these berries and you will recover. Also have a certain Medicine Man and Woman make a medicine that they know about. It will help make you well again.'"

The Medicine Man and Woman made the medicine. Handsome Lake took this medicine and was made completely well. The three men said, "There are four of us. The fourth spirit or angel will visit you at the time of your departure form this earth. We are here to tell you how the Great Spirit wants his people to live on earth. He speaks to you through us. We, the Four Messengers, will deliver the words and wishes of the Creator of all things. You are to deliver our message to the Red People on the earth. Through us, the Four Messengers, the Great One will tell you what is right and what is wrong on this earth. You are to deliver His message to your people.'

"It is the time of the Strawberry Thanksgiving. Tell your people to continue, as of old, the ceremonial Thanksgiving songs and dances such as are performed certain seasons of the year."

The Messengers said to Kaniatario, Handsome Lake, "Look and see." Handsome Lake looked and saw a valley between two hills. Hot vapor and steam was coming from a deep pit in the valley. The Messengers said, "Buried in that pit is an earth man. He must remain there forever, his punishment for refusing to deliver the message of the Great Spirit."

Handsome Lake said to the Council, "The Great One says you are to drink no more liquor! It was sent by the Evil Spirit to destroy the Indian. You must, when you hear this message, spill this poison on the ground and never touch it again.

"You must cease practicing witchcraft. Cease causing mental or physical illness. To do so is sinful.

"Some use certain charms to attract and influence people. Such methods are harmful to mankind. Destroy such and never employ them again.

"Some people, wishing to have no children, destroy them before birth. Such things must cease." He said, "A man and his wife live together and bear children.

"Sometimes a man leaves his wife and child for another woman. Such actions must cease. It is the command of the Great Creator.

"Man and wife must live together. They must rear their children well and keep them in good health. Their hearts must be filled with love for each other.

"Sometimes a man or woman become jealous of one another. Sometimes they even become jealous of the love of their children. Because of this they sometimes desert their children. Such a thing is sinful. Never desert your children. It is the command of the Creator." So said Kaniatario.

"A mother often becomes jealous of her son-in-law and causes trouble between her daughter and her daughter's husband. Sometimes this trouble even causes the married couple to separate and the home is broken up. Such actions on the part of the jealous one is sinful and must cease," said the Prophet.

"It is a sin for a father who has been drinking to play with his child. It burns the child's blood." So said the prophet.

"If a married couple have no children let them adopt from the wife's clan two or three children. The couple should rear and love them as their own," said Kaniatario.

Handsome Lake said, "Whoever is kind to the aged wins favor in the eyes of the Creator. Take care and love the old people and treat them as you would children. Never hurt their feelings by unkind words or actions.

"Adults should listen to children who are naturally honest and whose advice is often very good," said Kaniatario.

He said, "There is a special punishment after death for that man who is cross to his wife or who strikes her."

He said, "Some of you have been among white people and have seen their peculiar way of punishing a child by striking the child. Never break the spirit of the child. The Creator loves children and whoever whips a child, sins. As a punishment, blow water into a child's face. If the child still does not mind, threaten to throw him into the river."

Handsome Lake said, "A man is happy with his family life. He goes on the hunt to supply his family with food. In the forest he, the hunter, meets one who loves to gossip and who tells him that his wife is unfaithful while he is away hunting. The hunter is sad at heart and because of this evil gossip he deserts his wife. His footsteps head toward the house of his own clan or family instead of to the door of his wife's house. The Great One is sad because such gossip has caused all this needless trouble. Gossip is sinful and it causes bad feelings and trouble between friends. Such evil must cease. It is also sinful to listen to an evil tale and not try to stop it before it causes trouble," so said the Prophet.

"Never put food away when visitors come. Always invite them to sit down and eat. Share what you have with others, especially the poor and less fortunate. This pleases the Sky Father.

"The Great Father is happy when you call on a poor person who is ragged and unkempt. Wash the orphan's face and comb the orphan's hair," so said Handsome Lake. Kaniatario said, "If you see an orphan or poor child, always ask the child in and give it food. This pleases the Creator, who loves poor people and especially children." He said, "Give food and clothing to the needy." He said, "A person is good looking and boasts of it. A person is strong and boasts of it. A man is a good runner and is continually boasting that he can run like the wind or outrun a deer. To boast of such gifts is sinful. Instead, you must thank the Creator that he has given you these gifts. If you are so

fortunate as to have a special gift or talent use it to help your people, not yourself." He said, "It has been the Indians' customs to help each other during cabin-building time, corn-husking time, harvesting time, and in times of sickness. The Creator says to continue to carry on this custom. It is good to have helping bees." He said, "Help each other in time of need."

Kaniatario said, "The white people are all around you. The Indian is like a small island in a large river. To protect the Indians from the numerous white men, the Council of the Six Nations should appoint two young men from each nation to go to the white man's town. There, they should go to school and learn the habits and ways of the white people. So many white people surround us that we must learn their ways to protect ourselves.

"White people have a custom that is good. To protect his family in case of the father's death, he has a farm that will provide them with food. On this farm he raises cows, horses, and other stock. It is good that you adopt some of the things of the white men. It is good to have a nice garden and house. It is good to have cows, horses, pigs, and other livestock, providing there is no pride. It is possible to overdo this thing," said the Prophet. "Sometimes one will find a garden in the forest. He will help himself to the products of the garden without the owner's consent. To take what does not belong to you is sinful. If you really are in 'need,' ask the owner for some. The owner must not refuse if he has plenty." So said Kaniatario.

"There are certain animal and bird societies, Buffalo, Bear, Eagle, and Otter Societies, whose members have certain powers and aids because of the animals. It is the wish of the Great One that the members scatter tobacco and never meet again," said Kaniatario.

"Chiefs must remember that they are to work for the welfare of their people, not themselves. The welfare of the Nation must always be the first thought in the mind of a chief," said the Prophet. Handsome Lake said, "People must never forget to give thanks for life and the gifts from above. Thanks must be given for the things of the earth, upward to the sky." Kaniatario said, "There will become a day when the deer and the bear will become extinct. These animals have been used as sacred food at the ceremonial feasts. When the deer and bears are killed off, the people will use beef and pork as ceremonial food.

"You are not aware that the Evil Spirit is ever near you. He continually is trying to prevent you from attending the Ceremonies and Thanksgiving at the Long House. He will try to persuade you not to attend. Do not heed his advice. It pleases the Great One that you attend the Ceremonies held in his honor," said Kaniatario. "The One Above has created a new kind of deer. These deer are colored white. The male's coat is spotted and the female's coat has stripes on her side. These deer are sacred and are not to be killed," said Kaniatario.

He said, "The pigeon and the hawk do not mate. The Indian should marry into his or her own race."

He said, "There are three grades of sin: the sins of chiefs, the sins of the religious leaders, and the sins of the common people. The greater the office, the greater the sin.

"Chiefs and leaders must not quarrel, but must work together in peace and harmony," said the Prophet.

He said, "Some have laughed at the desires of the Creator. They have said that there is not harm in drinking strong drink. Let there be a contest between two groups of equal number. One group will eat food such as corn, beans, and vegetables. The other group will drink strong drink. Before the feast is over you will see that the group of the strong drink will have killed one of their own number while those who ate food only will be well and with clear minds."

He said, "Fear not the white man who surrounds you and who has his eyes upon you. The Creator watches from above and will protect the Red Children."

He said, "The Great One is angry at some of you. It is a grave sin for an Indian to make fun and laugh at the dances and ceremonials of his fathers. There is a terrible punishment after death for that Indian who is guilty of such a dishonorable thing.

"In the Upper World the Great One is sad. The Evil One says that man belongs to him because man does what the Evil One demands. The Evil One says that if he tells man to strike his neighbor that man obeys. From now on, you must not call the Great One our Ruler. He does not rule the would now. You must call him Our Creator. The Evil One you must call the Tormenter." So said the Prophet.

The Prophet said, "It is a sin to take another's life."

He said, "At the beginning of the planting season it has been the custom of the old people to have a virgin girl scatter kernels of corn over the new made hills of corn. This is to be done in the early dawn while the dew is yet on the earth and before the sunrise. As she does this she is to ask the Creator for a good crop of corn. This custom pleases the Creator.

"Do not fear death. When your time comes to leave this earth, sing your death song and die bravely, if you have led a good life upon this earth. If you truly repent your sins, you do not have to fear," said the Prophet.

"Because of outside influences, the Six Nations have become divided and disunited. Never again, upon this earth, will the Six Nations be united as of old," so said Kaniatario.

"The Creator gave the Medicine Men and Women their ability and gifts for the good of the people. A Medicine Man or Woman should give his or her service freely, asking only tobacco in payment," said the Prophet. "Before using a plant for medicine, scatter tobacco and thank the plant for its aid. Thank also the Creator. Plant seeds when you uproot the plant. It is wrong to pick any plant if you do not intend to use it," said the Prophet.

"Grief adds to the sorrow of the dead. It takes ten days for the spirit of a dead person to reach the Spirit World. At the end of ten days, prepare a feast in honor of the dead person. The spirit of the dead one will be at the feast. Cease grieving after the Death Feast," said Kaniatario. "In the sky there are four great roads. They are the paths of the four human races of the world. The trail of the dead is the Milky Way," said the Prophet. The Great Sky Trail stretches above the earth. He said, "The world will be destroyed by fire. Those who have been faithful to the Four Messengers will fall into a deep sleep. They will be lifted up to the New World. They will not suffer." He said, "It pleases the Creator when a hunter shares his kill with the needy, the widow, and the orphan." The Three Messengers took Handsome Lake along the Great Sky Road to visit the Land of Evil Souls and also the Land of the Good Spirits. Sprawled upon the Sky Road was a very fat woman. She was so huge and fat that she could not stand up on her feet. She clutched at everything in attempt to stand. The Messengers said that this woman, while on the earth, was very grasping and stingy. Because of her greed this is her punishment after death. "Those who gain their wealth through greed and dishonesty cannot stand on the sky road," they said.

He saw three groups of people. The largest group was the unbelievers. The next largest group was the half believers. The third group, a very small group, was the faithful. The Messengers said it would be this way. Beside the Spirit Road he saw a house with bars in the window, a pair of handcuffs, a hangman's rope, and a whip. The Messengers said that these will be for the Indians who think that the Indian Law is no good. He saw a long iron house. It was white hot. The house had one door and no windows. Many foot marks led in at the door. Many of them were moccasin tracks. He could hear sounds of wailing and crys of pain. This is the future home of those Indians who abandon the religion of their own fathers.

Below him he saw the Buffalo Creek Reservation. It was covered with a huge net. He said, "I believe that we will lose this reservation to the whites." It happened as predicted. The Three Messengers pointed toward the west, the setting sun. Handsome Lake looked and saw a white man prodding the earth with a bayonet. The Messengers said, "The white man wants you Iroquois to help him kill some of your own people who are fighting for their country. Tell your people that they are not to aid the white man in destroying Indian people. Half way on the Sky Trail the Prophet saw George Washington and his dog standing before a nice appearing house that hung from the sky. The white President seemed contented. They, the Messengers, said that because the Town Destroyer had allowed the Indians of the Six Nations to stay in their native lands instead of driving them to the west, that he was allowed to live here as a reward. He is the only white man who got that near the New World.

In the Upper World Kaniatario met Jesus Christ. Christ showed him scars left on his hands and feet, caused by nails being driven into them. He showed him a knife wound in his side. The wounds were raw and unhealed. Christ said that when he tried to tell his people, the white men, the wishes of the Creator, they killed him. He said that when the end of the world comes, they would stretch out their hands for his aid but that he would turn his back to them. He said to Handsome Lake, "Tell your people that they must not follow the ways of the white man."

Along the Sky Trail Handsome Lake saw a tired-looking man carrying earth and putting it in a huge pile. Such is the punishment for that Indian who sells the country, the birthright of his people, to the invader. He must move and put into a huge pile all of the land that he has sold. In the Upper World there was a wide, rough road of many foot marks. A small trail branched off from this. This small trail had a few foot marks, mostly of children. The wide road was to the land of the Evil One. The narrow trail led to the lodge of the Good Spirit.

Carrying a crystal that protected them, the three Messengers led Handsome Lake to the House of the Evil Spirit. The House of the Tormenter was long, made of iron and was hot. It was in this that Handsome Lake saw the punishments for the sinful—the lovers of alcohol, witchcrafts, the vain, wife beaters, gossips, quarrels, fiddle players, card players, etc.

The Three Messengers left the House of the Evil One. They followed the narrow trail of few foot marks. This trail led to the Land of the Happy Spirits. The trail led to a beautiful country. There were great trees, many bearing different kinds of fruits. Strawberries grew abundantly along the trail. Birds of all kinds filled the air with sweet music. Game was abundant. The animals seemed to live together in friendship. Kaniatario saw all these things.

Three places in the New World were visited by Kaniatario. They were the Spring, the Grassy Place, and the Place of Trees. He met his dog that had been dead for some time. The dog recognized Kaniatario and seemed well and contented. He saw his dead niece and son walking along together. Behind them were two long-dead elders. They all seemed very happy. He heard loud singing. It was the voice of a good man, long dead. It had been the custom of this man, while on earth, to call the people together to perform the feather dance. He was doing the same thing in the New World. He and the people all seemed well

and happy. Kaniatario's future home in the New World was pointed out to him. After showing Handsome Lake a little of the Upper World the Three Messengers led him back to earth.

Handsome Lake lived at Cornplanter Reservation for ten years, Cold Springs for two years, and Tonawanda for four years. While at Tonawanda the Onondagas, People of the Hills, sent a message to him requesting him to journey to Onondaga to preach the Kariwiio, the Good Word. The Three Messengers told Handsome Lake to go to Onondaga. They said, "While you are at Onondaga you will sing your Death Song, you will die." When Handsome Lake delivered his answer to the Onondagas, the children of the Senecas held a council and invited Handsome Lake to attend. Two representatives of the Child Council wept tears as they begged Handsome Lake to remain with them at Tonawanda.

Many people journeyed with the Prophet to Onondaga. Many tracks led there from Tonawanda. They travelled one sun and camped at the long-abandoned Seneca town of Ganowages on the Genesee River. That night Handsome Lake had a vision. He saw an old trail overgrown and covered with grass. At the end of the second day the party camped at a long-abandoned Seneca town near where the city of Geneva now stands. That night Handsome Lake had a vision. He saw a woman and she was speaking. When the party approached Onondaga, Handsome Lake was very ill. He was so ill that he could hardly stand. The Onondagas played a game of lacrosse, hoping to cheer him up.

Kaniatario said, "I will soon go to the New World. I see before me a plain pathway. Those who believe my message will follow in my foot-steps. I will welcome them with outstretched arms."

There, at Onondaga, the fourth Messenger came to lead Kani-atario to the New World. The date was August 10, 1815. Handsome Lake is buried near the Long House at Onondaga.

American Revolutionary War

At the outbreak of the Revolutionary War most of the Mohawks from Kahnawake, St. Regis, and Oka wanted to remain neutral. Many of them sympathized with the Americans. The Indian and especially the Iroquois who always had been a free people would lean toward any nation who was fighting for liberty and equality. One band of Mohawks in 1775, acting on their own, sent a delegation to General George Washington announcing their willingness to aid the Americans. The speeches of the chiefs of this delegation have been preserved. Rev. Samuel Kirkland, missionary to the Oneidas, acted as interpreter. One of the Kahnawake chiefs arose and said,

"I see a great war cloud rising in the east. This war cloud may make great trouble and bring much distress upon the American people. Because of this our very souls trouble us. War is a great evil to a nation and to the people.

"We Mohawks of Kahnawake know this by sad experience in the war between the English and the French by which the French were brought to ruin. We Kahnawakes rejoice to see the Americans have such independent spirits as to take up arms and defend their rights and liberties.

"We believe you will succeed because we believe that God is on your side.

"But we think that your liberty and freedom will be gained at the expense of much blood and great distress upon your people. The King of England is a powerful king or he would never have been able to conquer the French of Canada. But we think that the King of Heaven is stronger than any earthly king and will defend the oppressed."

"Brother Bostonians, be strong and courageous. Your cause is good. You will assuredly be supported by the Great Spirit above, whose omnipotent arm will defend you and in the end will give you a victory, a victory that will resound through all the world. The day of this victory will be a sabbath day to you and your children. It will be celebrated with joyful hearts as long as the true American spirit will beat in your breasts. Your true Indian friends of the north will do what they can in your favor. Indians are born free people.

"They love liberty, yes, they would wish to live as free as the deer in the forests or as the fowls of the air. Brother Bostonians, you are a great people and able to meet the King of England on the battlefield. We are feeble compared to what we were once. You will, I hope, always remember the old people who were once the lords of the soil, but who are now reduced both in number and in strength. But the war spirit is still in us. We will do what we can to aid you when the opportunity shall offer, even if it should result in the destruction of our village by the British, your enemies. Remember, Brother Bostonians, the words of your brothers of Kahnawake. Never forget that a portion of them are your friends at heart. They pray to the Great Spirit that you become a free people, as the Indians, your red brothers."

Much has been written about the raids of the Mohawks against the American colonies, so much that many are led to think that all of the Mohawks sided with England. It is a historical fact that there were many Mohawks, as well as other Indian tribes, who fought for the cause of the Americans. Many of the Kahnawake and St. Regis Mohawks as well as part of the Wolf Clan of Mohawks then living in the Mohawk Valley served as trustworthy scouts in the American Army. The Oneida, Tuscarora, Delaware, and other Indian tribes also served under General George Washington. Nearly one-half of the Iroquois served the patriots in the Revolutionary War. It was a Scatchicoke Indian who was Washington's personal bodyguard. Lieut. Nicholas Cusick, Tuscarora Indian, was the personal bodyguard of General Layfayette, great Frenchman who aided the Americans. Many other famous Indians made names for themselves by serving the patriots in a cause that they felt was just. It is unfortunate that most historians fail to record in their readings for young people the great sacrifice that many Indians made in their efforts to protect the Americans. Washington himself wrote, "If the Indians had been our enemies instead of our friends, the war would not have ended in American independence." It was the Oneida and Tuscarora Indians, both Iroquois tribes, who fed Washington's starving army at Valley Forge when the white settlers had refused him another kernel of corn.

Certain Mohawks, tired of war, wished to remain neutral in this great quarrel between the white men. One old chief voiced the thoughts of this group when he said,

"Once again the white men are fighting among themselves. They are fighting over the lands that they took from us. Why should we take sides in their fights? Long ago they encouraged us to go to war against our own people. Did they come to help us? They gave us weapons and encouraged our tribes to destroy each other. When we had become weak and our country was soaked with the blood of our people, they came and occupied our lands. Let the white men alone. Let them destroy each other. Perhaps when they have killed each other off, when they have gone, the forests, mountains, lakes, and rivers which the Great Spirit had given to our fathers will return to us."

A company of Minutemen was organized among the Stockbridge Indians of Massachusetts before the Lexington Battle and they were at the American Camp at Cambridge.

CORNPLANTER
AND HIS FATHER

It seemed the custom of the early fur trader, who, when living among distant tribes, would take an Indian woman for a wife. It seems also to have been a practice of these traders that they returned home from their business of gathering pelts to desert their Indian wives. Such a one was a man named John O'Bail, who was an Albany trader. He had fur trade relations principally with the Senecas, exchanging rum, guns, and other trade goods for peltries. O'Bail, after staying some years with the Senecas, became tired of his forest life, his Seneca wife, and his half-breed boy. He deserted them, returning to Albany where he married a white woman named Mary Kloats. Near Fort Plain on the Mohawk River, he settled down to farming life.

When his half-breed son, Gy-want-wa-ka, became older, he asked his mother why he was lighter than other members of the tribe. He was told that his father was a white trader who lived near Albany. This made young Cornplanter curious. Often he wondered what his father looked like and why he never came to see him or his mother. When Gy-want-wa-ka became a man he was a great warrior. His fame as a brave man spread far among distant tribes. During the Revolutionary War, settlers shivered at the mention of his name.

One August day in 1780, the father of Cornplanter, John O'Bail, was captured by Joseph Brant, War Captain of the Mohawks. With Brant were some of Cornplanter's Senecas. Cornplanter heard of the capture of his father and sent for him. When his shaking father stood before him, not knowing that Cornplanter was his son, he expected to be put to death. Cornplanter addressed him thus:

"You, I understand, are John O'Bail, once a trader among the Senecas. You are my father. My name is also John O'Bail or Gy-want-wa-ka, the Cornplanter. I am a warrior and have taken many scalps. You are now my prisoner, but you are safe from all harm! Go with me to my home in the Seneca country and you will be kindly cared for. My strong arm shall provide you with corn and venison. There my mother awaits you. But, if you prefer to go back among your paleface friends, you shall be allowed to do so, and I will send an escort of trusty Senecas to conduct you back to Fort Plain."

John O'Bail thought for a moment and decided that he would return to Fort Plain. The father of Cornplanter was escorted back to his farm by Seneca scouts and left near the fort.

Cornplanter later became a friend of the Long Knives, the Americans, and particularly George Washington. He is buried on the little Cornplanter Reservation in northeastern Pennsylvania.

HONAYAWAS

One hundred and fifty years ago there was a Seneca Reservation near where the City of Buffalo now stands. During the War of 1812 the Seneca Indians fought for the Americans. They were led by a famous Seneca war-chief called Honayawas. White people called Honayawas Farmer's Brother, because he was a friend of George Washington, a noted farmer. In the year 1814 just after the Battle of Chippewa, during the War of 1812, a Chippewa Indian was seen entering the white town of Buffalo. This Chippewa claimed that he deserted from the British army and wished to fight with the Americans.

Following the Indian custom of welcoming visitors, the Senecas accepted the Chippewa and welcomed him to their homes. They treated him as an honored guest. However, they suspected him of being a spy under the hire of the British.

All went well until the Americans started treating the Chippewa to alcoholic drink. Soon his mind and reason left him. Loudly the Chippewa boasted of the numerous scalps that he had taken. He bragged of killing many Americans. He bragged of even killing a close friend of Farmer's Brother. The Senecas who were with the Chippewa immediately sent for Honayawas who was with a wounded officer at the Phoenix Tavern in the town of Buffalo.

Leaving his sick friend, Honayawas, the old Chief, stalked down what is now the main street of Buffalo. Approaching the Chippewa warrior he seized him by the hair and with a mighty blow knocked him to the ground. Honayawas was then over eighty years old. The whites who stood watching did not try to stop Farmer's Brother. When the stunned spy recovered a little he sat up. Farmer's Brother held in his hand a rifle, a tomahawk, and a knife. He asked the spy which of these weapons he preferred to die by. The Chippewa chose the rifle as his death weapon. Holding the muzzle of the rifle against the spy's heart, Honayawas pulled the trigger. Thus was a spy executed in the then small town of Buffalo by Honayawas, a famous War Captain of the Senecas. Honayawas was respected by not only the Indians but by the white settlers as well. He never touched the white man's rum which had ruined many of his people. He was buried in Buffalo with high military honors by the United States Fifth Regiment. Honayawas' grave may be seen today, along with the graves of Red Jacket and other famous Senecas, in one corner of the Forest Lawn Cemetery in the city of Buffalo.

The War of the Revolution was over. George Washington sent Colonel Pickering and his agents to council with the Six Nations and to arrange for a treaty of peace. This council was held at Tioga Point, Oct. 25, 1790.

During the treaty, the people of the Six Nations indulged in games and held dances. The Americans gave the Indians six running pigs for capturing and cooking. The race for the pigs was long and exciting and the fun created by this gift caused friendly feelings between the people of the two races.

At the conclusion of the treaty the Senecas made plans to adopt one called Thomas Morris, of Philadelphia, into their tribe. A post was erected in the center of the dance ground. The Indians prepared to start the ceremony. That night the Americans, following their usual custom at treaties, circulated rum freely among the Indians. This unnatural drink greatly excited the young men of the Six Nations and at the height of the adoption dance it started the young Oneidas into boasting of their great prowess in battle and of their successes against the enemy while upon the war-path. The Oneidas had sided with the Americans during the Revolutionary War. The Senecas had fought as allies on the side of the British during the same war.

The Senecas at once resented these vaunts and boastings of the young Oneidas. Hands immediately flew to knives and tomahawks. The young warriors of the Oneidas and Senecas with hate in their hearts and showing in their eyes faced each other. In a flash the spark had caught and it looked as if bloodshed would follow.

In the crisis an aged Cayuga Chief, Fish Carrier, walked into the council circle. He struck the war-post in their midst a resounding blow and in a loud voice he exclaimed: "You are but a parcel of boys; when you have attained my age, and performed the warlike deeds that I have performed, you may boast what you have done; not until then." Saying this, the aged Chief threw down the war-post and ended the dance. The youthful warriors, Oneidas and Senecas, with shamed faces and downcast eyes, returned to their shelters in silence.

Among the Iroquois, a few words from a man of deeds will go further than all the stirring speeches of those who have no record of prowess to back up their threats and fiery denunciations.

Among the Iroquois, the wisdom of the aged was never questioned.

THE ONEIDA

The Oneidas are a branch of the great Iroquois Confederacy. They are called O-na-yote-ka-o-na or Granite People in their own language. They have also been known as The People of the Upright or Standing Stone. Some have called them the People of the Red Stone. Their National or Council name is Ne-ar-de-on-dar-go-wah or Great Tree. The French called them Onneiouts and the English called them Oneidas.

During the wars in Europe between the French and the English these two nations who had colonies in America spared no effort to get the different Indian nations in America to fight against their rivals in the New World. Both the French and the English desired the fur trade of the Iroquois and other Indian nations. Both the French and the English cast greedy eyes on the lands of the Iroquois. Both claimed the Iroquois country as their own. The Iroquois never admitted that either the French or the English had any claim over them or their country, as illustrated by a speech by Skadekanatie to Gov. Fletcher of Albany during May of 1764, an excerpt of which follows:

"You say that we are subjects to the King of England and the Duke of York. We say we are brethren, and take care of ourselves."

Skadekanatie continues to inform the English Governor:

"The privilege of meeting in General Council when we please is a privilege we always have enjoyed; no former Governor of the name of Corlear (New York State) ever obstructed this privilege. We planted a Tree of Peace in this place with them. Its roots and branches extend as far as Virginia and New England, and we have reposed with pleasure under its shade. Brother, let us keep to that First Tree, and let us be united and unanimous; such prohibition of our assemblies will be of ill consequence, and occasion differences between us."

Needless to say, York Colony was wise to see that they had better agree with the Onondaga speaker and let the matter rest if they valued their own safety. All English colonies had much to thank the Iroquois for protection against the French and their Indian allies. There is all truth in a statement by the Onondaga council to the Governor of York Colony concerning this Iroquois protection:

"Brother Cayenguirago (Gov. Fletcher)! When the Christians first arrived in this country, we received them kindly. When they were but a small people, we entered into a league with them, to guard them from all enemies whatsoever. We were so fond of their society that we tied the great canoe which brought them, not with a rope of bark to a tree, but with a strong iron chain fastened to a great mountain. Now, before the Christians arrived, the General Council of the Five Nations was held at Onondaga, where there has been from the beginning, a continual fire kept burning; it is made of two great logs, whose flames never extinguishes. As soon as the Hatchet Makers (Christians) arrived, the Great Council at Onondaga planted a Tree at Albany, whose roots and branches have since spread as far as New England, Connecticut, Pennsylvania, Maryland, and Virginia; and **under the shade of this tree all these English colonies have frequently been sheltered** (emphasis added)."

Tradition says that the Oneidas, after they had left the region of Oswego, settled on the banks of Oneida Lake where Oneida Creek enters. From there they gradually spread out moving east of Oneida Lake and forming their main village called Ga-no-a-lo-hale, meaning A Head On a Pole. Their several settlements covered the elevated lands at the heads of the streams bordering Oneida Lake. They were thus located when the whites first appeared in their country.

It is recorded that the Oneidas, as well as other Iroquois, were very friendly toward the white settlers from Europe. From the very first contact with white people, from the era of Henry Hudson in 1609 to the coming of the Dutch settlers to the Valley of the Hudson-Mohawk, they were on terms of the closest amity. When the English took over the Dutch colony, assuming sovereignty in 1664, the same close relations were continued. The Oneidas carried on an extensive fur trade with these early English settlers. This trade was uninterrupted and the peace was faithfully preserved by the Oneidas and the English colonies. Not a drop of blood was shed to disturb the hundred and more years of harmony.

The hospitality of the Iroquois is well known. To them it was a way of life and came as naturally as breathing. Many a poor white settler was aided by these first Americans. When the poor Palantine

Germans settled at Weisersdorf, New York, it was only through the kindness of the Iroquois, who showed them how to find food in the forest and who gave them of their own stores of food, that the little colony survived. When their little ones cried for food, it was the Oneidas who gave them meat, corn, and bread. The English and Dutch settlers were likewise aided by the Iroquois. Says a historian, Francis Drake, of the Oneidas, "Brave in war, mild in peace, and hospitable under all circumstances, no visitor or wayfarer, white or red, ever entered their cabins without having his wants supplied and being kindly put on his track."

The Moravian missionary, Rev. John Heckewelder, who labored among the eastern Indians in 1762 says of Iroquois hospitality:

"They think that the Great Spirit made the earth and all that it contains for the common good of mankind; when he stocked the country that he gave them with plenty of game, it was not for the benefit of a few, but for all. Everything was given in common for the sons of men. From this principle, hospitality flows as from its source. With them it is not a virtue, but a strict duty. Hence they are never in search of excuses to avoid giving, but freely support their neighbors' wants from the stock prepared for their own use. They give and are hospitable to all without exception, and will always share with each other and with the stranger, even to their last morsel. They rather would lie down themselves on an empty stomach than have it laid to their charge that they had neglected their duty by not satisfying the wants of the stranger, the sick, or the needy."

Canassatego, a noted Iroquois, once told the English that the Great Spirit long ago had said to his fathers: "Nourish and instruct your children as I have nourished and instructed you. Be just to all men, and kind to strangers that come among you. So shall ye be happy, and be loved by all and I myself shall sometimes visit and assist you."

At different periods in their history the Oneidas adopted and gave lands to refugee tribes. The Tuscaroras, Stockbridges, Brothertons, and Canestogas were among such adopted peoples. The Oneidas gave the Tuscaroras lands between the Unadilla and Chenango Rivers. The Mohekunnuks were given land a few miles south of

Oneida Castle. South of Clinton, New York, the New England Indian refugees were given land and protection.

But acts of hospitality and kindness were not the only gifts of the Indian, and particularly the Iroquois, to the man from Europe. Says Dr. William B. Newell, anthropologist and historian, of the way of life of the Iroquois and its effect upon the early aliens coming to these shores from Europe:

"We know that many Iroquois sociological and philosophical ideas were taken to Europe with the first contact made with the American Indian. After the first 250 years, sufficient exchange had taken place to definitely establish new cultural traits which have given birth to new ideas heretofore unknown in the Old World. A discussion of the moral and ethical values of Indian culture would require a volume in itself. **Indian political theories as embraced in the League of the Iroquois are important and stand out in marked contrast to the European theory of the 'Divine Right of Kings' which flourished in Europe at the time of the discovery of America** (emphasis added). The individual rights of man were recognized in America long before the Europeans awakened to this political philosophy. Ideas of freedom, liberty, and equality existed and were engraved in the hearts of the Iroquois when Europeans were boiled or roasted alive for daring to speak against the state or church. One of the outstanding differences between the European and the American Indian was the fact that in America the Indian was permitted freedom of thought while in Europe an individual's thinking was done for him by autocratic and dogmatic leaders. A similar situation still exists in some European countries, and even in America there are those who would shape our opinions if they could. Governor Cadwaller Colden who wrote the first American history in 1727, some fifty years before the Revolutionary War, tells us that these Iroquois men were elected on the basis of their merit, because of their honesty and integrity, and that they were usually the poorest men in the nation; never keeping anything for themselves, but distributing all annuities and monies equally among the people. It was from this first history that the early colonists were informed that here existed a true democracy. **"Present day Americans are doing these Iroquois Indian things which were strange to**

them before coming to the land of the free and the home of the brave (emphasis added)."

"Among the Iroquois, dictators were unknown. No man could tell another what he must do. Every man and every woman was allowed freedom of expression. Every person was allowed to decide for himself what he should do. Even the sachems and chiefs suggested but never commanded or insisted too strongly. To do such a thing would immediately lower them in the estimation of the people and cause their removal from office. 'We counsel together' was a famous phrase of the Iroquois."

Says a modern writer, Felix S. Cohen, formerly of the United States Department of Interior:

"Out of America came the vision of Utopia and particularly from the Iroquois government, where government might rest upon the consent of the governed, rather than upon the divine right of kings or religious leaders, where no man could be dispossessed of land he used for his sustenance. Politically, there was nothing in the kingdoms and empires of Europe in the 15th and 16th centuries to equal the democratic constitution of the Iroquois, with its provisions for initiative, referendum, and recall, and its universal suffrage for women as well as men. American Democracy, freedom, and tolerance are more American than European and have deep aboriginal roots in our land. Francisco Vitoria, teacher of Moral Theology at the University of Salamanca, in 1532 and Hugo Grotius, both weavers of the fabric of modern International Law, were deeply influenced by Indian examples of just government. In the American Revolution, the French Revolution, and in the revolt of the Spanish Colonies, the passion for liberty nourished by the Indian burst into consuming flame."

Again this authority writes:

"Racial mystics among English historians are fond of attributing the traditions of civil liberty in America to reactionary medieval documents like Magna Carta or to the traditions of freedom-loving Englishmen, who had endured centuries of Tudor, Stuart, and Plantagenet despotism. Under the influence of modern theories of race and climate, it has been fashionable to trace the roots of American freedom to the Anglo-Saxon inhabitants of dark German forests, most of whom were serfs. These historians forget that there were free men in America before the first white settlers arrived with their slaves and indentured servants. There is more truth in a popular account of America widely circulated in Great Britain in 1776: 'The daring passion of the American is liberty and that in its fullest extent; nor is it the original natives only to whom this passion is confined; our colonists sent thither seem to have imbibed the same principles.' Truly the passion for liberty as practiced by the Iroquois was a contagious thing.

"In these and many other ways Iroquois Indian America helped to civilize Europe (emphasis added). Is it any wonder that the greatest teachers of American Democracy have gone to school with the Indian? It was the great Iroquois Chief, Canassatego who gave the American Colonists some advice which was one of the first steps in the long story of the American Revolution. It was this chief who said to the colonial governors meeting at Lancaster in 1774: 'Our wise forefathers established Union and Amity between the Five Nations. This has made us formidable. This has given us great weight and authority with our neighboring nations. We are a powerful Confederacy; and by your observing the same methods our wise forefathers have taken, you will acquire such Strength and Power. Therefore whatever befalls you, never fall out with one another.'

"Franklin plainly had the Iroquois Confederation in mind when he drew up his plan of Union to be presented at the Albany Congress. The author of our first Bill of Rights freely acknowledged his debt to Indian teachers. Comparing the freedom of Indian society with the oppression of European society, Thomas Jefferson struck the keynote of the great American experiment in Democracy."

Said the Commissioners from Congress (General Schuyler) to the Six Nation Council, August 25, 1775:

"Our wise forefathers said to one another, 'The Six Nations are a wise people. Let us harken to them, and take their counsel, and teacher our children to follow it.' Our old men have done so. They have frequently taken a single arrow, and said, 'Children, see how easily it is broken. Then they have taken and tied thirteen arrows together with a strong string, and our strongest men could not break it. 'See,' said they, 'that is what the Six Nations mean. Divided, a single man may destroy you. United you are a match for the whole world.'"

The Iroquois Republic was a federation of Indian states holding general power, while each state was guaranteed independence and sovereignty. At the same time, each man and woman was guaranteed equal rights. The idea of a confederation as we have seen was suggested to the United States by the Six Nations. North of the United States, the Canadians got the same idea from their United States neighbors.

An enemy of the Iroquois, Monsieur De La Poterie, in his *History of North America* said of the Iroquois:

"When we speak of the Five Nations in France, they are thought by a common mistake to be mere barbarians, always thirsting after human blood; but their true character is very different. They are indeed the fiercest and most formidable people in North America, and at the same time are as politic and judicious as can be conceived; and this appears from the management of all the affairs which they transact, not only with the French and English, but likewise with almost all the Indian nations of this vast continent."

From W. C. Brant's notes on the Iroquois, October 9, 1884, we read:

"That great incentive to eloquence, patriotism, was not lacking to these Ciceros of the wilds. No nation of which we have a record was dominated in a larger degree by this lofty sentiment. They were proud of their history and their achievements, devotedly attached to their institution, and enthusiastic at the mention of the long line of chieftains and sages who, from the era of Hiawatha, had assisted in erecting their grand Indian empire. **The time will come when the institutions, polity, eloquence, and achievements of this remarkable people will be themes of study for the youth in our schools of learning** (emphasis added). The unvarying courtesy, sobriety, and dignity of their convocations led one of their learned Jesuit historians to liken them to the Roman Senate."

The Revolutionary War took the Iroquois by surprise. They had always stood as firm friends of the English government and of the English people. When some of these same English people, now rebels against England, began to talk against the Mother country, the Iroquois were at a loss as what to do, who to listen to. Samuel Kirkland, a Christian missionary, had been among the Oneidas for many years and the Oneidas were very fond of him. They had often followed his advice. He had banished strong drink from among them and was regarded as their friend. Often he had told them to honor the great English king across the sea. Now, with the war approaching, this same missionary told them that the king was bad, that he was a very selfish, unreasonable, and cruel man. It is no wonder that the people of the Six Nations were confused and bewildered. The Iroquois have never been good at the art of "Double Talk."

Because they remembered the "Chain of Friendship" made with the English over a hundred years before the Revolution they, being an honest people, hesitated to take sides with the Americans. At the same time, being a freedom-loving people, they hesitated to fight on the side of England. They tried hard to remain neutral, thinking that in time the quarrel between the American colonies and their mother country would be settled peaceably.

The Oneida Nation, speaking for the entire Six Nations, sent the Americans an Iroquois Proclamation of Neutrality. Their message to the Americans was as follows:

"Brothers and leaders of New England: Some of our younger brothers, the New England Indians, have settled in our vicinity. We have pitied them and have given them refuge, allowed them to settle on our lands where they may live in peace. The are going back to their original country (now occupied by white people) to bring here parts of their families that were left behind. We hope that they may visit their friends and return here to their settlements in peace. We are taking this measure because of the disagreeable situation of affairs in your country and we ask God that they may return in peace.

"Brothers, the Governor and Chiefs of New England: May your minds be at peace respecting the Indians of the Six Nations. You and England are two brothers and we cannot interfere in your quarrel which seems unnatural. You are two brothers of one blood. We love both you and Old England and we do not wish to join either side in such a contest. If the English King across the sea asks our aid we will refuse to help him. If your colonies ask our aid, we shall refuse it also. We Indians are confused and bewildered at what has happened. The present situation of you and England, two brothers, is new and strange to us.

"We have thought back on our history and cannot find in the traditions of our ancestors a similar instance of such a strange thing.

"Brothers: Possess your minds in peace and do not become angered at any of us Indians because we refuse to join in the contest. We are for peace and always have been.

"Brothers: If it were an outsider, a foreign nation who had attacked you, we would look into the matter as we have done in the past. We have always come to your rescue when such an event happened. We hope through the goodness of God that your trouble will soon be removed and that the dark clouds of war will be dispersed.

"Brothers: We have told you our minds and our minds are for peace. We desire that you do not ask our brothers, the New England Indians, for their assistance in your war. It is the desire of the Six Nations that we Indians be all of one mind and live with one another, and you white people settle your own disputes between yourselves.

"Brothers: We have now told you the thoughts that are in our hearts. We would like to know your thoughts on this matter."

There is no doubt that the Iroquois wished to remain neutral but, as history proves, the white nations have always used the Indians as tools in all of their wars. History also shows that the Indian allies were never given a consideration or thanks at the end of any of the white man wars.

Says Jasper Hill, a noted Delaware of today, concerning this trait of European races:

"Most of the so-called Indian wars and massacres that happened during the early colonial period can be traced directly to the result of either French, English, or American influence. It seems that none of these 'civilized nations' were high-minded enough to scorn availing themselves of Indian scouts and warriors to do the dirty work for them. They would not dare to risk their 'Christian reputations' by doing it themselves. These cold and hard facts have been too long ignored by the white historians when they are spewing forth their habitual estimate of the barbarous ferocity of the early Red Man."

In all of their wars the colonies of New England made a practice of soliciting Indian aid. All of the American colonies were concerned as to what the Iroquois Confederacy would do in case of a break with England. It has been said that the New England Colonies desired the rich Iroquois country and that they had attempted to turn the mother country against the Iroquois in the hope that they would profit by such a move. Because of a land grant made by an English King, the Massachusetts Colony claimed all the lands west of their colony, all the land clear to the Pacific Ocean. Iroquois country would lie within that grant; a generous King indeed. People today often wonder why the Americans, while organizing the Boston Tea Party, dressed in the costume of the Mohawks. One authority says that they dressed and painted like Mohawks because they hoped that England would blame the Mohawks for the tea being dumped into Boston Harbor and that she would declare war against the Mohawks. Naturally the other Iroquois would join their Mohawk brethren in such a fight. This scheme would be a means of driving the Iroquois from the desired country or it would make them so weak that it would be an easy task for the New Englanders to drive them from their country. The New Englanders were old hands at uprooting and dispossessing Indian peoples. Had they not preached from the pulpit that they were God's chosen people, sent here to America to destroy the heathen Indians?

The New England Indians, those few who were left, were greatly influenced by the whites of that section. Many of them, crowded out by the invaders, left their New England country and sought refuge in the lands of the Iroquois. Many of them settled in the Oneida country where they were in a good position to influence the Oneidas. A speech of a New England Indian to the Massachusetts Congress gives a hint of this influence and may partly explain why the Oneidas, when they did join in the war, took the side of the Americans. This influence, as well as the strong influence of Rev. Samuel Kirkland, had a great deal to do with the decision of the Oneidas.

Captain Solomon Ahhaunnawaumut to Provincial Congress of Massachusetts:

"Brothers: Long ago you lived far to the east beyond the great waters. When you first came to our county you were a very small people. You were little and weak and we were great. We welcomed you because we took you for a friend. We kept you under our arms and protected you against all who would harm you. There were no quarrels between us and we were true friends. But now our conditions are changed. You have become great and powerful. You reach to the clouds. Your voice is heard around the world. I have become very little. I am not as high as your heel. You now look out for me and I look to you for protection.

"Brothers: We are grieved to hear of this unnatural quarrel between you and Old England. It seems that only the shedding of blood will end this quarrel. We could never understand what caused this quarrel between you and the country you came from.

"Brothers: As we are brothers I shall help you all that I can. Whenever I see your blood running, you will see me ready to avenge the injury done my brother. Although I am very small, I will grip hold of your enemies heel, that he cannot run so fast and so light as he could if he had nothing there.

"Brothers: I want your advice as to what I am now going to say. We think it wise before action starts to travel to the west to find out what our Indian brothers of the Six Nations think of this quarrel. We would like to know how they stand, whether they are for you or for your enemies. If we find that they are for England, we will try to change their minds. We think that they will listen to us as they have always turned to us whenever they wished to know of events that happened to the eastward. We have advised them on all that concerns important news that comes from the rising sun. If they listen to us you will not have to worry about danger that comes from that direction. Whichever way they think I will tell you. We feel that we can better help you in this way than by marching off to Boston and staying there. Blood may not flow for a long time. I leave this to your consideration whether to leave immediately for Boston or to wait until the blood flows.

"Brothers: We want you to know that we are not falling back on our engagements. We are always ready to help you and come to your relief. We shall be guided by our advice and counsel."

The Iroquois informed both the Americans and the English of their desire to remain neutral. They begged both countries to keep the war from the territory of the Iroquois, and that an army marching across their soil would be considered an unfriendly act, that in all likelihood it would cause their young men to take up arms.

Their efforts were hopeless and when an American army under General Schuyler advanced through the Mohawk country, it was met by a delegation of Iroquois who told them to turn back. They guaranteed that Sir John Johnson, the British Indian Agent, could cause no trouble by influencing them. Part of their speech is here given:

"Brothers Attend! It was your request and a matter agreed upon by the Twelve United Colonies that we Iroquois should mind nothing but peace. Therefore, Brothers, as we mean to observe that agreement, we have expressed ourselves above, and as brothers, we mind nothing but peace. We look upon ourselves as mediators between two parties; therefore, brothers, as your messengers declared that you would not be the aggressors, we informed Sir John (British Indian Agent) of this, and earnestly begged of him not to be the aggressor, or the means of spilling blood; and at the same time assured him that if we found that he should be the aggressor, we would not pay any further attention to him; and likewise told him that if our brothers of the United Colonies were the aggressors, we should treat them in like manner."

It did not take the Iroquois long to realize that both white groups did not intend to leave their country out of the war. Perhaps it would have been impossible as the country of the Iroquois was in the very center of the two peoples. Their lands lay in the very path that an invading army would have to travel over. One Indian compared his people to a piece of cloth between a pair of scissors, the scissors being the contesting white people, the Indians the cloth that was being cut. Such was to be the case and it was not the first or the twentieth time that the Indian found himself in that position.

England used every method to incite the Iroquois against the Americans. The United States did not hesitate then, or in all of her wars, to use the Indians to fight her battles. Both sides made many promises to the Indians for their aid, promises which neither white nation kept after the war was over and the aid of the Indians was no longer needed.

On May 25, 1776, Congress resolved: "That it was highly expedient to engage the Indians in the service of the United Colonies," and they empowered the Commander in Chief to employ in Canada and elsewhere Indians, offering them a reward of a hundred dollars for every commissioned officer and thirty dollars for every private soldier of the British troops that they should take prisoner. Congress also authorized Washington to employ the Indians of Penobscot, St. Johns, and Nova Scotia, who offered their services. Both sides offered scalp bounties but the English went a little farther; they offered a larger reward for scalps than they did for prisoners, thus making killing more profitable.

There were many Indian tribes who helped the cause of the Americans. The Delaware Indians were promised that if they aided the struggling colonies, that after the war an Indian state would be added to the original thirteen states and that the Delawares would be at the head of it. The Delawares believed this and many of their men fought and died for the colonists. We all know the facts! They are not difficult to find if one cares to look for them! The faithful Delawares did not get their Indian state. They were not even permitted to become Americans or given permission to live beside their white brothers. Instead they were driven from their country. Over fifty treaties were made with the Delaware Indians alone and all fifty were broken by the United States. Some of the Delawares were even driven beyond the Rio Grande River into Mexico! But let us turn to the Iroquois and particularly to the part of them called the Oneidas.

As the war progressed the Iroquois found themselves in a very trying position. Pressure from both white groups was put on them. Long before this time they had forgotten the use of the bow and arrow. They now depended upon the powder, shot, and other European commodities for their very existence. If these things were kept from them by either England or America, the end would not be far off. It was either fight for one or the other, or die!

At a great council at Onondaga, the capital of the Six Nations, they talked over the problem. Some were for helping Great Britain because of the Treaty of Alliance made with her so many years before. Besides, had not the Americans broken the Treaty of Fort Stanwix and crowded them from their lands? England promised them that in case Great Britain lost the war, that the Six Nations would be given an amount of land in Canada equal to that lost in their present country. The Oneidas and Tuscaroras, members of the Iroquois League, due to the influence of Rev. Kirkland and the Christian New England Indians who had settled in their country, did not want to fight the Americans. The white men had not yet reached their lands and crowded them off as they had done to the Mohawks. In order for the Iroquois to officially declare war it was necessary for every state in their union to declare war. According to the Iroquois Constitution it had to be unanimous.

Council after council was held but all would not agree as to what policy to follow. The Mohawks were for war. The Onondagas were neutral. The Senecas were lukewarm to either side. The Oneidas and Tuscaroras sympathized with the struggling colonies. Even within a nation all could not agree. Finally Thayendinagea, a Mohawk leader said, "Let each nation be responsible for its own members. Let each tribe decide for itself what path it will take in this war."

The Oneidas from the beginning resisted the war measure saying that it was unwise and not practical. Their opposition defeated the war measure as an act of the League. Says Morgan, noted anthropologist in *League of the Iroquois*, "If the League had been unanimous as under its ancient law, if they had been unanimous against the Americans, it is quite likely that Burgoyne's Campaign would have been a British triumph and that the war would have ended in the success of the Royal arms."

The Oneidas sided with the revolting colonists and remained with their allies throughout the war. They shared the respect and esteem of General Washington. The Oneida Chiefs and people stood by him in the darkest and most dangerous days of the Revolution. During the war the Oneidas took no scalps nor did they harm women, children, or old people. The Oneida warriors were among the best scouts in the United States Army and they were very useful throughout the war.

They were of outstanding service in observing the progress of every British army from Canada.

These Iroquois showed great personal bravery and on one occasion they saved the life of General Lafayette. The Oriskany Clan of Oneidas joined General Herkimer on the day of his disastrous battle. They were led by their chiefs, Colonel Honyerry and Cornelius. They fought with great skill and bravery throughout the day.

Congress applauded the Oneidas for their firmness and integrity and assured them friendship and protection for all time to come. The Oneidas, Stockbridge Indians, Delawares, Kahnawakes, Tuscaroras, and other Indians were in Washington's camp. On April 9, 1779, Congress passed a resolution granting Commissions of Captain to four Oneidas and eight Commissions of Lieutenants. The Oneida Chief Atayataroughta was commissioned a Lieutenant Colonel. Other commissions were issued to Oneidas during the course of the war.

Oneidas made great sacrifices during the war. In 1779 British troops burnt their homes, destroyed their fields of grain, and cut down their orchards. The brave people were reduced to poverty, want, and dependence. They were forced to flee down the Mohawk Valley and for awhile lived in the vicinity of Schenectady, New York. They were long in recovering from their depression. Their reward from the "generous" United States was an amount of money that averaged about fifty cents a person. This was their payment for the destruction of their homes, corn fields, orchards, and for cutting themselves away from their Iroquois brethren. In the end, the Oneidas fared no better than did their brethren who fought for England.

As for the Iroquois who had fought and died for Great Britain, what was their fate? After the war was over and their beautiful country was laid to waste and ashes, they journeyed to Oswego, the supply base of Great Britain. There, at Oswego, they were informed that their services were no longer needed and their supplies and provisions were stopped. This was the base ingratitude that the English at Fort Oswego showed their faithful allies. The English Government showed the same ingratitude when at the Treaty of Peace between themselves and the American Colonies they made no provision nor asked any for the Iroquois who had served them so faithfully. All of their former

promises were forgotten. The Indian owners of the very regions over which so much blood had been spilled were not consulted in any of the transactions. Their rights were totally ignored! From the Revolutionary period on, the Iroquois were to see bitter times. They were to be buffeted from pillar to post. Their lands and those things that they held dear, even the graves of their fathers, were to be taken from them until they would hardly have a place that they could call their own. As a famous Seneca, Ely Parker, once said, "While living they are not let alone—When dead they are not left unmolested!"

The Oneidas were not long to enjoy the country that they had fought so hard to keep. Almost immediately after the war, greedy land speculators cast their eyes on the rich Iroquois Country. When one reads the records of the methods used by these big land companies and when one knows how the government allowed their faithful allies and friends to be robbed, one cannot but feel angered and ashamed.

The "Preemptive right" to purchase the Iroquois lands has a long and crooked trail. Under the grant from King James I of England to the Plymouth Colony, Massachusetts claimed the Iroquois Country. By agreement between the white people this land claim exchanged hands several times until it was obtained by a few land companies, the most dishonest of which was the Ogden Land Company, an unincorporated association. A brief outline of the methods used by this company will give the reader a little light on how the Iroquois and other Indian nations lost their few remaining acres, because the methods used by this company were similar to all land companies of that day.

Says Morgan in *League of the Iroquois*:

"To embitter their sense of desolation as a nation, the 'Preemptive right' to these last remnants of their ancient possessions is now held by a company of land speculators, the Ogden Land Company, who, to wrest away these few acres, have pursued and hunted for the last fourteen years, with a degree of wickedness hardly to be paralleled in the history of human avarice. Not only have every principle of honesty, every dictate of humanity, every Christian precept been violated by this company, in their eager artifices to despoil the Iroquois; but the darkest frauds, the basest bribery, and the most execrable intrigues which soulless avarice could suggest, have been practiced, in open day, upon this defenseless and much-injured people. The natural feelings of man and the sense of public justice are violated and appalled at the narration of their proceedings. It is no small crime against humanity to seize the firesides and the property of a whole community, without an equivalent, and against their will; and then to to drive them beggared and outraged into a wild and inhospitable wilderness. And yet this is the exact scheme of the Ogden Land company; the one in which they have long been engaged, and the one which they still continue to prosecute the Georgia Treaty with the Cherokees, so justly held up to execration, in a white page, compared with the Treaties of 1838 and 1842, which were forced upon the Iroquois."

To make one land swindle, the Senate of the United States passed an act to destroy the Iroquois Government by abrogating the Iroquois Law of Unanimity of All before a sale could be made. The land company then proceeded to purchase the votes of a majority of chiefs. Ten chiefs were paid $30,000 in bribes. Others were given liquor until they were intoxicated and then made to sign. Others were made chiefs by a sham election and then their signatures were taken. Others who were not chiefs were bribed to sign the treaty as chiefs. It was known by the United States Government that fifteen-sixteenth of the people, almost the entire nation, were unwilling to sell. At this particular swindle, the Iroquois struggled for justice, yet the Senate ratified the treaty! In most of these so-called land sales the Iroquois received a few cents an acre!

In 1790 General Washington had said to the Six Nations, "In the future you cannot be defrauded of your lands. No state or person can purchase your lands unless at some public treaty held under the authority of the United States. The General Government will never consent to your being defrauded; but it will protect you in all your just rights. You possess the right to sell, and the right of refusing to sell your lands. The United States will be true and faithful to their engagements."

At the Canandaigua Treaty of 1794 these same promises were solemnly made again by the agents of the United States to the people of the Six Nations.

Thus we see how the American Government bartered away its integrity to minister to the greedy demands of a few already rich individuals, heads of land companies, and this over the protest of many of their own white citizens!

Some of the speeches of the Iroquois telling of the reasons why they desired to remain in their own country are sad enough to move a heart of stone. The following, one of many that have been recorded, is Red Jacket's speech to a Mr. Richardson who requested that the Iroquois sell their right to the reservations in the Holland Land Purchase:

"Brother! We open our ears to the talk you lately delivered to us at our Council Fire. In doing important business it is best not to tell long stories, but to come to it in a few words. We therefore shall not repeat your talk, which is fresh in our minds. We have well considered it, and the advantages and disadvantages of your offers. We request your attention to our answers, which is not from the speaker alone, but from all of the Sachems and Chiefs around our Council Fire.

93

"Brother! We know that great men, as well as great nations, have different interests and different minds, and do not see the same light, but we hope our answer will be agreeable to you and your employers.

"Brother! Your application for the purchase of our lands is to our minds very extraordinary. It has been made in a crooked manner. You have not walked in a straight path pointed out by the great council of your nation. You have no writings from your great father, the President of the United States. In making up our minds we have looked back and remembered how Yorkers purchased our lands in former times. They bought them, piece by piece, for a little money paid to a few men in our nation, and not to all our brethren—until our planting and hunting grounds have become very small and if we sell them, we know not where to spread our blankets.

"Brother! You tell us your employers have purchased of the council of Yorkers, a right to buy our lands. We do not understand how this can be. The lands do not belong to the Yorkers; they are ours, and were given to us by the Great Spirit!

"Brother! We think it strange that you should jump over the lands of our brethren in the east, to come to our Council Fire so far away, to get our lands. When we sold our lands in the east to the white people, we determined never to sell those we kept, which are as small as we can comfortably live on.

"Brother! You want us to travel with you and look for new lands. If we should sell our lands and move off into a distant country toward the setting sun, we should be looked upon in the country to which we go as foreigners and strangers. We should be despised by the red as well as the white men, and we should soon be surrounded by the white people, who will there also kill our game and come upon our lands and try to get them from us.

"Brother! We are determined not to sell our lands, but to continue living on them. We like them. They are fruitful and produce corn in abundance for us for the support of our women and children, and grass and herbs for our cattle.

"Brother! At the treaties held for the purchase of our lands, the white men, with sweet voices and smiling faces, told us they loved us, but that the King's children on the other side of the lake would cheat us. When we go to the other side of the lake, the King's children tell us your people will cheat us. These things puzzle our heads, and we believe that the Indians must take care of themselves, and not trust either in your people or in the King's children.

"Brother! At a late council we requested our agents to tell you that we would not sell our lands, and we think you have not spoken to our agents, or they would have told you so, and we should not have met you at our council fire at this time.

"Brother! The white people buy and sell false rights to our lands, and your employers as you say, paid a great price for their rights. They must have plenty of money to spend it in buying false rights to land belonging to Indians. The loss of it will not hurt them, but our lands and homes are of great value to us, and we wish you to go back with your talk to your employers, and tell them and the Yorkers that they have no right to buy and sell false rights to our lands.

"Brother! We hope that you clearly understand the things we have told you. This is all that we have to say."

At another time Red Jacket said to agents of the Ogden Land Company:

"We first knew you as a feeble plant, which wanted a little earth to grow upon. We took pity and gave it to you, and afterward, we could have tread you under our feet, we watered and protected you. Now, because of our help, you have grown to be a mighty tree, whose top reaches the clouds, and whose branches overspread the whole land. While we, who were once the tall pine of the forest, have become the feeble plant, and we need your protection . . . When you first came to our country you clung around our knee and called us father. We took you by the hand, lifted you up, and called you brother. You have grown faster that we, so that we can no longer reach up to your hand, but we wish to cling around your knee and be called your children . . . Anon," pointing to some crippled warriors of the 1812 War among the Indian listeners and blazing with anger, he continued, "It was not our quarrel!

"We knew not that you were right! We asked not! We cared not! It was enough for us to know that you were our brothers. We fought and bled for you and now," pointing to some Indians who had been wounded in the war, "dare you presume that our father, the President of the United States, while he sees our blood running yet fresh from the wounds received while fighting his battles, has sent you with a message to persuade us to relinquish the poor remains of our once boundless possessions—to sell the birthplace of our children and the graves of our fathers? No! Sooner than we believe that he gave you this message, we will believe that you have stolen your commission, and are a cheat and a liar!"

What sorrow in the speech given by the Iroquois, December 2, 1790, addressed to Washington and complaining of a fraudulent purchase:

"Father! You have said that we are in your hands, and that by closing it you can crush us. Are you determined to crush us? If you are, tell us so, that those of our nation who have become your children, and have determined to die so, may know what to do. He would ask you to put him out of pain. Another, who will not think of dying by the hand of his father, has said that he would retire to the Chautauqua Region, eat of the fatal root, and sleep with his fathers in peace. Before you determine on such a measure so unjust, look up to God, who made us as well as you!"

What truth in the words of a famous Iroquois, Big Kettle, to the Government of the United States, "When your Thirteen Colonies won their freedom from Great Britain, you took a brand from our fire and kindled it. Now the same fire is trying to consume the very people who taught you the worth of such a fire."

But there were valuable interests at stake for the rich land companies since the market value of land in New York State depended entirely upon removal, so they said, of the Iroquois. New pressure was bought to bear upon the government to have the Indians sent westward. Efforts were made to deceive the Iroquois into thinking that if they moved west they would receive in exchange for their lands the same amount that they would lose in the state. During the summer of 1819 desperate efforts were made to induce all of the Six Nations to migrate but, led chiefly by Red Jacket, they fought the move.

The Oneidas were more pliable, owing to a division in their ranks because of the Christian religion which had been lately introduced to them. Ever since the missionary, Eleazer Williams, had worked among them they had been divided into two parties, Followers of the Old Way and the Christians. The Christians placed all of their faith in Mr. Williams' advice. They had great confidence in him and followed his every suggestion, material as well as spiritual. Some Indians have believed that Williams was sincere in thinking that the Oneidas would be happier in Wisconsin. On the other hand there is evidence that he was under the hire of Ogden himself. It is known that Williams was at first very strong against removal. In 1817 he definitely opposed removal and resisted all of the efforts of De Witt Clinton who wanted him to use his influence and advocate removal before a general council of the Six Nations. Clinton, Ogden, and certain religious leaders tried to persuade the Indians to move west.

General E. A. Ellis wrote concerning Williams (*Annual Report of the American Historical Association*, Vol. 1, 1906):

"He (Williams) was full of vagaries that would account in part for his easy seduction by the New York land speculators."

Again they record:

"At New York he was in long consultation with Thomas Ogden, Esq., chief manager of a New York land company. Mr. Ogden conceived that Williams would be a powerful agent in effecting the removal of the Senecas, and from him Mr. Williams received a good sum, several hundred dollars in money. These largesses were repeated by Mr. Ogden several times after."

After the first removal attempt failed, Thomas L. Ogden became chief proprietor of the preemptive right. He tried to force the Iroquois to move, even going so far as to survey their land prior to any sale saying that if they did not sell, the government would force them to leave anyhow.

The Oneidas had surrendered most of their lands until finally all that was left was one small reservation. Still they were not even allowed to keep that. Their lands were invaded by the whites and even the government was constantly egging them to part with these last few acres, those acres that they had been told they could keep for all time to come. They clung to their old country in New York State as long as possible. But the lands were coveted and the cry increased for their removal to the west.

It must be remembered that the Oneidas at this period were not living by hunting and fishing. They were excellent farmers and had large fields of corn and other agricultural produces, herds of cattle and other livestock, as well as large orchards. Their homes were well framed houses or cabins as good as those of their white neighbors. They had turned their attention to the cultivation of the soil and had abandoned the chase for the surer supply of domestic animals. Here was a community of several thousand human beings, human people, living in a community larger than many of the farming villages of New York State, all living in their own houses, cultivating from fifty to a hundred acres of land, their children attending church and school and yet the white settlers and the Ogden Land company officials clamored for their removal saying, "It is for their interest to remove! They will find good hunting and fishing grounds in the west! Make way for civilization! The Indians stand in our way, we the cultivators of the soil. Civilization must go ahead! The hunter state! Yak! Yak! Yak! etc." The Ogden officials and the white brothers apparently did not remember, or perhaps they did not want to remember, the accounts of the great fields of corn and other products of the soil, the well-framed houses, the well-kept orchards that General Sullivan had destroyed, burnt to the ground, when he marched through the Iroquois County during the Revolutionary War. Apparently they forgot the reports of Sullivan, especially where he records the thousands upon thousands of bushels of corn, the largest corn ever seen by white men, that were destroyed by his soldiers. They, the Iroquois, had turned their attention to the soil centuries before Columbus was born and the Indian since that time had given the European settlers many valuable lessons in agriculture. They, in fact, were better farmers than the first whites who came to the shores of America. Yet the cry was shouted until the sound echoed through the walls of government, "They stand in the way of progress! They must be swept out!"

In 1819 Williams had gone to Washington saying that he represented the Iroquois and that they were anxious to move west. Then

Williams and a delegation, fourteen in number, claiming to represent the Iroquois-Oneidas, St. Regis, Stockbridges, Onondagas, Senecas, and Tuscaroras went to Wisconsin to see lands. It must be understood that the only Iroquois who had agreed to go west was the first Christian Oneida party. The one Onondaga, one Tuscarora, one Seneca, and Williams claiming to represent St. Regis went without authority of their tribes, on their own responsibility. They had no authority from their nations. In fact, the Iroquois emphatically expressed themselves as being against removal from their old homes which were surrounded by New York State.

The white settlers, largely of French blood, who lived at Green Bay did not want the Iroquois to move to Wisconsin. Apparently they had their own eyes on the Indian lands of Wisconsin. They tried very hard to persuade the Wisconsin Indians not to sell any land to the Indians of the Six Nations. However, the Menominees and Winnebagos sold them land on Fox River. Williams returned to New York after the transaction was made. He received the congratulations of De Witt Clinton and the curses of the Old Time Oneidas who begged the Rev. William Lacy of Albany to intercede for them with Bishop Hobart to have Williams removed from his office as missionary teacher. All of the other Iroquois showed their sentiment of disapproval (*Annual Report of American Historical Asso.*, Vol. 1, 1906). Nevertheless, though all of this was known to him, President Monroe, unhesitatingly gave his personal sanction to the agreement.

Naturally all of the Iroquois were in a very excited state of mind at the thought of losing their country. The New York State speculators tried to sell them the idea that the government was going to force them to give up their lands and go west. After a third treaty with the western Indians, the land companies redoubled their efforts to force the Iroquois to give up their country. They tried every trick known to break the power of Red Jacket. Several hundred Indians did finally migrate. Some went as far as Kansas where most of them died of sickness and starvation.

Among the reasons why the Iroquois did not want to leave their country was their natural love of their native soil. They regarded as holy their ancient country, the land that held the dust of their fathers. They knew that their lands must be very valuable from a white man's viewpoint. They realized that the title to the Wisconsin lands was far from clear. The Menominees had refused to admit the validity of the contracts of 1821 and 1822.

The poor, tired Oneidas were not long to enjoy their settlement or the church that they had worked so hard to erect. They dreaded leaving their old homes, their ancient lands, and the graves of their fathers. At their last council in New York State they were told that they already had agreed in 1831 to sell their country when the President of the United States wished to purchase. This, naturally was not true. This unjust clause had been fraudulently inserted after the treaty was signed and it was added without the knowledge of the Indians! They were totally against moving. However, in 1823 their removal from New York was decided upon. They were led by Eleazer Williams.

As they looked for the last time at the beautiful country that they were to see no more, their hearts were torn and crying.

It is hard for a member of the white race, who come from a race of globe wanderers, to realize the feelings of an Indian who is being torn from his home and country. As the Oneidas traveled into the sunset their thoughts were of the country that they had lost.

The words of Washington and the Thirteen Colonies echoed through their minds—the same "double talk"; familiar talk since the coming of the Hatchet Makers (Dec. 3, 1777):

"Brothers, Oneidas and Tuscaroras: Hearken to what we have to say to you in particular. It rejoices our hearts that we have no reason to reproach you in common with the rest of the Six Nations. We have experienced your love, strong as the oak, and your fidelity, unchangeable as truth. You have kept fast hold of the ancient covenant chain, and preserved it free from rust and decay, and bright as silver. Like brave men, for glory you despised danger; **you stood forth in the cause of your friends, and ventured your lives in our battles**. While the sun and moon continue to give light to the world, we shall love and respect you. **As our faithful and trusty friends, we shall protect you, and shall at all times consider your welfare as our own** (emphasis added)."

Yes, these were the words of Washington and of the Thirteen Colonies, these were the thoughts of the Oneidas as they looked for the last time on the lands of their fathers!

They were allowed 65,000 acres of land in Wisconsin in consideration for giving up their lands to New York State. Their country in Wisconsin was a valley or strip of land nine miles wide and twelve miles long, situated a few miles west of Green Bay, Wisconsin. The little river that ran through their reserve was called Tah-lon-ga-wa-nay (Place of many ducks). They called Green Bay Haw-ha-la-lik-Ong-gay (Home of many Men).

The Oneidas were very poor when they arrived in Wisconsin and they suffered great hardships. Before they could plant any corn, the land had to be cleared of the forests. They had to start from scratch and it was not the first time that this had happened to Indians. They had much to contend with. They mourned for their old country, their rich gardens, and fruit trees left behind.

It was not long before the white men were again trying to force their removal. There were at that time (1853) white men at Green Bay who tried to debase the Oneidas with every means in their power. Their reason for this was to make the Iroquois appear bad in the eyes of the government at Washington. These people, as usual, coveted the lands of the Oneidas. It was very fertile and had rich groves of timber on it. To obtain possession of this land they were eager to drive the Oneidas into the wilderness again. These people sent false tales to Washington making it appear that the Oneidas were a troublesome scourge to the white people and a nuisance to the settlers of Green Bay. "They must be removed!" was again the cry. The Indian agent appointed by the government worked hand in hand with the Green Bay land speculators and he even threatened and intimidated them. They were not only troubled with this problem but their crops failed and their people faced starvation. They were forced to sell their wood.

The agent informed them that they had no right to sell the wood, that it did not belong to them. He informed them that if they sold the wood, they would be removed to the west. This agent even made a trip to Washington with false tales in order to have the Iroquois removed. He might have been successful if it had not been for the aid and help that the Oneidas received through their missionary who protected and fought for justice for the Oneidas. Through their good and loyal missionary the plot of the Green Bay land speculators and the crooked agent failed. Be it recorded here that the missionaries to the Oneidas, after they had moved to Wisconsin, then and now, have ever watched out for the welfare and protection of their Oneida People. Often times it was they alone who held back the evil tide that would have crushed and killed them. One has but to watch the eyes of the faithful Episcopal priest and his co-workers, the Sisters of St. Anne, as they look on the Oneida children—to realize that the welfare and happiness of their little Indian flock is the foremost thought in their minds. One has but to look into the eyes of each little Indian boy and girl, as they talk to their priest and to the Sisters of St. Anne, to see love, confidence, and faith expressed there.

These loyal friends stuck to the Oneidas to the last, through all of the difficult times of the Oneida People. The Oneidas were never to be left in peace as history proved. The following is a copy of a letter written in the diary of Rachel Hill, an Oneida woman:

"I never cared much about making this church nice, for I've always thought we should have to leave it some day. In our old home in York State we had a nice church and nice homes, too, orchards and all we wanted but we had to leave all and come off here in the thick woods to suffer and lose everything. Now we are beginning to be comfortable, but see how our great father (the United States government) wants to get our lands. See how the white folks want to get our homes. We were rich once. We had large annuities and much land, and now this little piece is all we have left. I should think white folks would be ashamed to take this land away too. Why are there so many greedy white folks when they have Bibles and ministers and prayer books and churches and schools?"

A letter received from a young Wisconsin Oneida friend, dated April 13, 1949, will perhaps briefly explain the later history of the Oneida Indians of Wisconsin since their removal to that section of the country:

"Sago Akwesasne Brothers!

"I had a very enjoyable visit with you at the Oneida Festival in Wisconsin last July.

"Kindly take me as an example, if you will, of the average Oneida of my generation, for reasons self-explanatory in following paragraphs.

"My years are creeping near 30 and I speak very little of the Oneida language. I understand very little more than I speak. In 1932 and 1933 I saw the only two Indian ceremonies that my people had, I believe, during my lifetime and up until the time your group came to Oneida. Even they could hardly be called Indian Ceremonies. Very, very few people were capable of taking part save several aged men and women, who in their feeble years, exhibited complete Native abandon in their dancing, though feeble it was. Not many others took part, the youngest dancer being 40 years in age. Pathetic, isn't it?

"In my years in the grades I learned beadwork from the Stockbridge band of the Mohegan-Munsee Indians of Massachusetts who have a reserve about 60 miles north of the Oneidas in Wisconsin. As a Boy Scout in an Indian school I learned to dance and I loved it. We danced the Winnebago and Chippewa dances, for we, the Oneidas, had forgotten our dances. So also had we forgotten our ancient history. I carried my hobby of Indian handicraft through high school except for basketry, which I was forced to give up just as I was beginning to learn the hobby from grandmother. She passed to the Great Beyond at that time, and there was no one left to teach me.

"When did I first hear the story of Deganahwideh? In 1948 from the Akwesasne Mohawk Counselor Organization! And that is the first time that any of us here had heard of it, of the great league of our people, organized for everlasting peace. Pathetic? I'll say! It was then we realized how little we knew of our history. It was then that we knew we had a wonderful history, that we should hold our heads high!

"What are we going to do about it? We all sit looking at each other and wondering who is going to get up and speak his piece. No one moves. Why? Don't they care? Are they ashamed? Are they just too bashful and afraid of being laughed at? Or is it that they just lack leadership? Well I am going to do something about it. I am going to learn our culture and history and I am asking your help in this matter. I will then try to help my people to have a better understanding of their own culture. I will try to organize a club here in our Oneida community, an organization copied after your society. Such an Indian organization will help us to gain back to our people some of those things that we have lost, our language, a knowledge of our history, our pride!

"I will give you a brief account of our history. Since our separation from the New York Oneidas: We pooled money and trusted the government (then a bunch of two-faced, black-hearted land sharks) to purchase a reservation. This they did in Kansas. When our Oneida delegation arrived at our Kansas homesite, they found barren wasteland and would not accept. Instead, they asked for their money so they could do their own 'shopping.' But the government said, 'It will take some time, and if you are really in earnest we suggest you take up another collection.' This we did, and bought our present location in Wisconsin from the Menominees, who then moved north to Shawano.

"No word came from the government, so my Great-Grandfather, a tribal chief, took action. (He was a lawyer but was never brought to the bar because he refused to take out a citizenship.) The reply was, as the records were also, 'padded,' to show that it was government money which bought the Kansas land. Then about 1900 the government re-allotted our reservation to all people 6 months old and older with the condition (dictated—not agreed upon) that the land would be non-taxable for 25 years. This was called the Trust Period, at the end of which we would become citizens automatically and would pay taxes as white people. My Great-Grandfather and my Grandfather both read the original agreement which said the lands shall be non-taxable forever. Period. It was later padded, unknown to the Indians, once they had the signatures. Mother was notified in May, 1928, that Mr._____ now owned her 40 acres and she cried. The white settlers had only to pay three years taxes amounting to about $.50 per acre per year, and they took over. That was the end for us. Grandfather fought to the day of his death in 1942 at the age of 99 years. He was the last to fight. _____, one of our own tribe, took up the case, and was 'paid off' and beat it with the pay-off money as well as ours. _____, an Oneida from New York did likewise. Every lawyer we had won two or three hearings overwhelmingly, was 'paid off,' and took flight. Mr. _____ also from New York not only took the money but grandfather's treaty books.

"The best we can hope for now is to remain organized as a citizen community and try to gain back our history, our culture, and ideals and to preserve them. We must do this! We at least can keep our pride.

"In closing this letter I extend every good wish for good health and good luck to you and to your people. May we see you here again and soon.

"Sincerely, your Oneida Brother _____"

This Oneida history would not be complete without giving a brief history of a group of Oneidas who moved to Canada. After the Revolutionary War a considerable number migrated to Canada and settled on the Grand River. When those who were left in New York State migrated west to Wisconsin there was a number of them who were reluctant to go so far west. They desired to remain nearer their other Iroquois brethren. They sent deputations to Upper Canada in 1838 and 1839 to inquire as to whether they could secure land there. They were permitted to acquire 5,000 acres in the Township of Delaware in the County of Middlesex. In the fall of 1840 about 200 of the Oneidas came over and settled on this land that they had purchased from the white settlers. Another delegation of Oneidas followed in September 1841. In 1848 there were in all 436 Oneidas located on the 5,000 acre reservation which had been purchased for them with their own money. In 1856 they purchased another 400 acres of land and their reserve today consists of 5,271 acres. Since that time they have more than tripled in population. They are known as the Muncey Oneidas of the Thames River.

CHIEF SKENANDOAH, THE ONEIDA

Skenandoah, The Deer, was a famous Oneida chief. Skenandoah was always the warm and unwavering friend of the Americans.

The first settler of Whitesboro was a Mr. White. He, his wife, and little daughter lived in a lonely cabin many miles from any pioneer settlement. There were many Oneida Indians living in the vicinity of Mr. White's home. Mr. White had often smoked a pipe with the Indians and had always acted friendly toward them. Yet, the Oneidas look on him with suspicion. The did not exactly trust him and wondered at his friendship. They wondered if he was as sincere as he acted, if he really was a friend and good neighbor of the Indian people as he claimed to be. They decided to test his friendship.

Skenandoah, one of the leaders of the Oneidas, went to Mr. White's house. He said, "I have come to ask you to let your little daughter visit my cabin. I want her to know our people. I would like to take her home with me tonight."

The mother of the little girl was frightened. She was about to refuse the request, but the father smiled and said, "Yes, we would like to have our daughter visit you and your family. We are pleased that you have taken an interest in her. She should meet and play with her little Indian neighbors, your children. You may take her home with you."

Mr. White knew that it would have been useless to have refused the invitation. If the Oneidas, who were numerous and brave fighters, wanted to kill them anytime, it would be easy for them to do so. It would be useless to resist. He saw that it might do much good to grant the request as he did. He had acted as a good neighbor to the Indians and his friendship had been sincere.

The Oneida chief took the little girl by the hand. He said, "Tomorrow when the sun is high in heaven, I will bring her back." Together, the little girl and the Indian leader walked down the trail and disappeared into the forest.

The poor mother could not sleep that night. Not knowing anything of the true character of the old Indian, she feared the possible fate of her child. She was up early the next morning and watched, almost without hope, the trail that led to the Oneida settlement.

Slowly the Sun rose above the forest. When it reached the noon mark, the mother heard a happy childish laugh coming from down the trail. She looked and saw her little girl, still holding the hand of Skenandoah, coming from the woods. Her little daughter was all decked out in feathers, beaded moccasins, and Indian costume. With a happy cry the mother ran to meet them.

From that day on, the Oneidas were their friends and fully repaid the trust which the father had put in them.

Skenandoah was described by those who knew him as a tall, intelligent-appearing man of great physique. He was a man of great eloquence and good judgment. During the Revolutionary War he believed in the cause of the people of the United States and on more than one occasion warned his white neighbors of British invasions. It is known that he saved the people of the settlement of German Flats by giving them timely warning. He and his warriors fought on the side of the Americans in all of their border wars along the Mohawk River and surrounding territory. Trusty Oneida scouts were sent among the British in Canada and secured valuable information concerning the numbers, strength, and movements of the British. Skenandoah and his warriors fought beside General Herkimer in the battle of Oriskany. General George Washington commended his services. It was he and his Oneidas who saved Washington's starving army at Valley Forge by bringing him several hundred bushels of corn. Years before this, May 28, 1754, Oneidas under the leadership of the great Iroquois, Tanacharison, had helped Washington fight the first battle of his career, against the French under their commander, M. De Jumonville. It is just possible that they saved Washington's life in that battle as the English fired in great confusion. John Davidson, the Indian trader who was in the action afterward gave an account of the fight and he gave Iroquois full credit for doing most of the execution that was done. This incident is mentioned to point out just how much the United States owe the Iroquois.

In 1775, while on an official visit to Albany in behalf of his people, Skenandoah was given liquor. He became drunk and the next morning found himself in the gutter along one of Albany's streets. Everything of value had been taken from him including most of his clothes and chieftainship regalia. He was so chagrined and humiliated that he resolved never again to become intoxicated, a determination from which nothing could ever move him. On one occasion he said to his people, "Drink no fire-water of the white people! It makes you mice for the white men who are cats. Many a meal that have eaten of you!"

During old age he became blind and almost helpless. Just before his death he said to his people, "I am an aged hemlock. The winds of a hundred winters have whistled through my branches. I am dead at the top. The generation to which I have belonged has run away and left me. Why I live, the Great Spirit only knows." Skenandoah died at Oneida Castle, New York, on March 11, 1816, reputed to be 110 years of age.

In spite of all that the Oneidas had done for the cause of the Americans, in spite of British troops destroying their villages, crops, and orchards, and in spite of the fact that Congress applauded the Oneidas for their firmness and integrity, assuring them friendship and protection in their lands, after the war their hunting and fishing grounds—their lands and orchards—were invaded by the whites who sent up a clamor and increasing cry for their removal to the west. The poor, tired Oneidas were not long to enjoy their settlement that they had worked so hard to keep. They were totally averse to moving and leaving their old homelands and the graves of their fathers. Greedy land speculators, who coveted their lands, won out and it was in 1823 that their removal from New York was decided upon. Their trail to the west was wet by tears as the Oneidas left their beautiful homeland and the graves of their fathers.

Old Skenandoah had fought and died in vain!

SHIKELLAMY,
ONEIDA CHIEF, VICE-REGENT,
SUSQUEHANNA TRIBES

Shikellamy's real name was Ongwaterohiathe (It has caused the Sky to be bright for us).

When a tribe was conquered by the Six Nations, a deputy or vice-regent was sent by the Iroquois or Six Nation council to watch over the tribe. Shikellamy was such a deputy sent by the great Federal council of the Six Nations in 1728 to watch over the Delaware, Shawnee, and other tribes in the Valley of the Susquehanna River in what is now the state of Pennsylvania. This old chief was highly respected, by not only the Six Nations, but by the white colonial officials as well. He was always the friend of the white man and upon every occasion treated white settlers with great kindness. He never drank the white man's fire-water because, as he once said, "I never wish to be a fool." He tried to prevent the sale of this cursed drink to those Indians under his trust. One of his first acts as vice-regent was to send word to the colonial officials that unless they stopped peddling rum among his people, friendly relations between the Six Nations and the colony of Pennsylvania would cease. This ultimatum to the Pennsylvania government was delivered in 1731. Because of the harm that liquor peddling was causing among his people, many Indians were moving west to the Ohio Valley where the French were trying to alienate them from English interests. The English had reason to fear friendly relations between the Six Nations and the French.

Shikellamy was asked by the English to go to Onondaga to invite the Six Nation Chiefs to go to Philadelphia, the object—to secure the friendship and alliance of the Six Nations in case of war with France and also to try to get the Ohio Indians to return to the Susquehanna country to act as a bulwark against the enemy of the English. Though they mistrusted the English, three of the Six Nations sent delegates to the council in 1732. At Philadelphia the English were very concerned and uneasy as to whether the Six Nations were their friends or whether they would favor the French. They were put at ease by one of the speakers of the Confederacy who informed them that the Governor of Canada told them at council that he intended to war upon the English colonies and wished them to remain neutral. The Iroquois speaker then answered the French Governor:

"Onondiio, (Indian name of the French Governor) you are very proud! You are not wise to make war with Corlear (Indian name of the Governor of New York Colony) and propose neutrality to us. Corlear is our brother. **He came to us when he was little and a child**. We suckled him at our breasts. **We have nursed him and taken care of him till he has grown up to be a man** (emphasis added). He is our brother and of the same blood. He and we have but one ear to hear with, one eye to see with, and one mouth to speak with. We will not forsake him nor see any man make war upon him without assisting. We shall join him, and if we fight with you, we may have our own father, Onondiio, to bury in the ground. We would not have you force us to this, but be wise and live in peace!" (*Pa. Col. Records*, Vol. 3)

In the execution of his office Shikellamy conducted many important embassies between the Six Nations and the government of Pennsylvania. It was through this chief that the treaty of 1736 was called at which delegates from all of the Six Nations were present at the council hall in Philadelphia. Over a hundred Iroquois attended this council. At this meeting the Iroquois deeded to the State of Pennsylvania all of their Susquehanna lands. When most of the delegates had returned home, and several weeks later, another deed was drawn up by the whites and those Indians who had remained (most of them drunk) which signed away lands owned by the Delaware Indians. Because of this act, the Delaware and other Indians sought the

alliance of the French, and from 1755 to 1764 Pennsylvania was drenched in the blood of an Indian war. Old William Penn, a sincere and honest man, never stooped to crooked dealings with the Indian people. His sons, however, were not of the same make as their father but were more interested in personal profit and trickery. The results of this shameful act was one of the bloodiest wars in colonial history.

Because of the help of Shikellamy in cementing a friendship between the Six Nations and the Colony of Pennsylvania, a future nation, the United States of America, was made possible. If the Six Nations and the French had formed an alliance, there can be no doubt that the result would have been the destruction of all of the English colonies on the coast. Shikellamy was the mediator between the Colony of Pennsylvania and the Six Nations. He was the key to the friendship of the Iroquois!

Old Shikellamy became ill with fever and passed away Dec. 6, 1748. Said the Moravian missionary, Zinzindorf, of Shikellamy:

"He was truly an excellent and good man, possessed of many noble qualities of mind, that would do honor to many white men, laying claims to refinement and intelligence. He was possessed of great dignity, sobriety, and prudence, and was particularly noted for his extreme kindness to the inhabitants with whom he came in contact."

America owes much to this great Iroquois!

MIGRATION OF THE TUSCARORA

This story is about the Tuscarora Indians, the Wearers of Shirts.

Many or heap

winters

and summers (years)

in the past, (arrow going backwards)

the Wearers of Shirts, the Tuscarora,

owned a beautiful country. To the west of their land was the Appalachian Mountains. To the east of the mountains was the forest and grass-covered Atlantic Coastal Plain. They had wide rivers in their country. The sea, with its many fish, lay to the east.

Their dwellings were large and were made of bark, as in other Iroquoian villages.

They had rich soil in their country and were good farmers. They raised corn, beans, squashes, and other Indian garden products.

Many (a heap)

deer and other game lived in the forests of the Tuscarora Nation.

Fish swam in the rivers and the people caught many of them.

Many birds such as the duck and goose lived in the Tuscarora country.

In the olden days there were great forests of pine and other trees.

They lived in a land of plenty. There was always plenty of meat on the meat-drying racks.

In those old days when the Tuscarora Indians lived in their beautiful country now called North Carolina, they were a happy people. The sun shone in their hearts.

But black heart, sorrow, was to come to these peaceful people. Their hearts were to be filled with pain and a dark cloud.

From the rising sun across the

great salt water of the Atlantic Ocean

came a great winged canoe.

The canoe carried strange people with pale skins. They were hungry and asked for food and shelter of the Tuscaroras.

The white man found friends, not enemies, among the Tuscaroras. The Tuscaroras fed and sheltered these early white people who came to live among them. The Tuscaroras smoked the Pipe of Peace and Friendship with these white strangers.

The Indians gave the white settler

land to plant corn on for their women and children and showed them how to raise the corn, bean, and squash plants.

115

They gave them skins to make new clothing for their children.

When famine walked among the white settlers, it was the Tuscarora Indians who brought them meat, corn, and fish.

But from the rising sun

across the great waters.

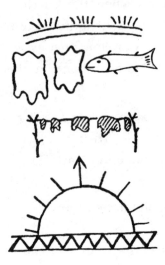

came many other white strangers. These newcomers were greedy and they carried weapons of war and destruction with them. Their hearts were black (cruel) and their tongues were crooked as the rattlesnake

They had no love for the Tuscaroras who had befriended them, but in their hands held a knife soon to be covered with blood, the life blood of the Tuscarora people.

With their axes they cut down the forests leaving nothing but blackened stumps where once great trees had stood.

With their guns that made noise like thunder, they killed that which the Indian depended on for his existence—the deer, bear, and other game.

Many of these newcomers hunted Tuscarora people. Not only did they hunt men, but women and children as well. They were slave traders and they had their eyes on the gold that the Tuscarora slaves brought from the Spanish plantation owners in the West Indies.

Strange, unknown diseases now swept among all Indian peoples. The Indians had no resistance against these diseases brought over from Europe. Smallpox, malaria, whooping cough, lung trouble, and other diseases swept many of them to death.

Many Indians died from the curse of alcohol.

Fear was in the hearts of the Tuscarora People. They fought desperately against the English of North Carolina in defense of their homes, their wives, and their children. The invaders with superior weapons and greater numbers defeated the Tuscarora People.

The remnant of the Tuscaroras packed their goods on their backs and headed towards the Great Bear, the north wind.

They were welcomed and sheltered by men of the Five Nations who had organized a confederation of peace. These Five Nations were the Mohawks, Oneidas, Onondagas, Cayugas, and Senecas. Their central council fire burned at Onondaga.

The official emblem of the Iroquois Confederacy was the Great Tree of Peace (white pine). The Tuscaroras took shelter beneath this Great Tree of Peace whose roots spread in four directions, north, south, east, and west, as an invitation for all peoples to join the league. On the topmost branch of the Great Tree perched the eagle, the guardian bird of the Five Nations. The Tuscaroras accepted this invitation and smoked the Pipe of Peace and friendship.

The Tuscaroras became the sixth nation of the Iroquois Confederacy.

The People of the Upright Stone, the Oneidas, gave the Tuscaroras a part of their country.

This gift of the Oneidas was the hunting and farming country between the Unadilla River and the Chenango River near where they flow into the great Susquehanna River.

During the Revolutionary War, the Tuscaroras fought and died for the Americans.

At Unadilla their towns were burned by the British. (During the War of 1812 they were again allies of the Americans.) After the Revolutionary War, the American settlers again demanded the country of the Tuscarora.

Some Tuscarora warriors were on a fishing trip at the west end of the Beautiful Lake (Ontario).

They found a land with many clear springs. There was plenty of game and many nut trees.

Their head man said, "Come, let us move to this new country, for the strangers seek our lands at Unadilla."

Once again the Tuscaroras packed their belongings on their backs. They migrated toward the setting sun.

They left the beautiful hill country given to them by the People of the Upright Stone. It was soon occupied by the strangers from across the salt waters.

Not far from the Great Falls (Niagara Falls) which makes the noise like thunder,

they erected their cabins and there they live to this day.

A Few Laws of the Iroquois Government

Wampum Law: It is provided thus —The War-Chief of the Oneidas shall be selected and appointed to his position by the women of the Clan of Odatseghdeh and shall be installed according to the Ceremony of Installing the Sachems. The title of the War-Chief of the Oneidas is Kanonwahdironh.

Wampum Law: It is provided thus—Shononghseseh, Thonaeghkenah, and Hahtyadonnentha (Turtle Clan) are the first party of the active counsellors and Odatseghden, Kahnondwenyah, and Tehyonhakwendeh are the Second Party (Wolf Clan). Tehyahtahontenyonk, Kahnyadaghshayen, and Honwatshadonneh are the Third Party (Bear Clan). The Third Party listens and watches over the proceedings, actions, and progress of the Council or discussion of the First and Second Parties. If an error occurs during the discussion, they, the Third Party of Sachems are to call attention to it and explain the same. When a question is decided right and sanctioned by the Third Party of the above mentioned Sachems, it has passed the Oneida Council. All three clans must agree before it is a law.

Wampum Law: It is provided thus—The business of the Confederate Nations shall be transacted by two combined groups of sachems, first the Mohawks and Senecas and second, the Oneidas and Cayugas. And in all cases, the decisions and resolutions of the Confederate Council shall be referred to the Firekeepers, the Onondagas, for final decision, or confirmation.

Wampum Law: It is provided thus—The decision of each body of the combined Sachems must be unanimous. Before referring the subject by a speaker to the next body of Sachems and if they agree unanimously, the business is reported to the Firekeepers for confirmation and their confirmation is reported to the Mohawk Sachems, to declare or not the decision of the question or matter in council.

Wampum Law: It is provided thus—If a difference arises between the combined Sachems in the Confederate Council, on any question, and they agree to refer the question or difficulty to the Onondagas, the Firekeepers, for decision, then the Firekeepers shall determine and decide which would be the most advantageous to the people, and in such case their decision shall be final.

Wampum Law: It is provided thus—Whenever there is any question under consideration by the council of the two combined groups of Sachems who have agreed unanimously to the question and it is referred to the Onondaga Council for confirmation, if in the opinion of the Onondagas their decision is thought to be ruinous, injurious, and disadvantageous to the people, then the Onondagas must refer the question back to the combined Sachems for consideration, mentioning the points objected to. Then the combined Sachems shall reconsider the question and when corrected or amended, the question shall again be referred to the Firekeepers who will sanction or confirm the law.

Wampum Law: It is provided thus—If any of the War-Chiefs of the Confederate Nations act contrary to justice in the capacity of his position he shall be deprived of his title by the women of his clan or by the warriors of his clan and they will appoint another to take his place. Either the women or the men may act alone or co-jointly in the matter.

Wampum Law: It is provided thus—That if a Sachem disregards the third warning from the women of his clan for any error or wrong-doing, then said women shall refer the matter to the War-Chief. The War-Chief shall then address himself to the offending Sachem in the following manner and words,

"So you, (naming the said Sachem), disregard and set at naught all the warnings of the women of your clan Wahsehnenhsawenradeh, therefore behold the bright light of the sun and in the sun's light and brightness, I have to dispossess you of the sacred emblem or title to your office. I now take off from your brow the deer antlers which are the emblem of your office and token of your nobility and I now discharge you and therefore hand over to the women of your clan your forfeited title of nobility, for it is their heritage."

The War-Chief shall then address the women of the clans of the deposed Sachem thus, "Gwanisdenhokonah, Mothers, as I have now discharged your Sachem, so now I have to hand back to you the title of Lordship, therefore repossess it."

Again addressing himself to the deposed Sachem he shall say,

"As I have now deposed you and discharged you, so you are no longer Sachem. You shall now go your own way alone. The rest of the Confederate People shall not go with you, as we do no know what manner of spirit possessed you. And, as the Great Creator will not have anything to do with sin, so he will not come to take you out of the place of destruction, Jiyodenhwenjiyakohn, and you shall never be restored to the position you once occupied."

Then the War-Chief shall address himself to the Sachems of the nations to which belonged the deposed Sachem and he will say,

"Know ye, my Lords, that I have taken the deer antlers from off the brow of (naming the deposed Sachem) which was the emblem of office and token of his nobility." And the said Sachem shall have no alternative but to sanction the same.

Wampum Law: It is provided thus—That the Sachems of the Iroquois Confederacy shall be the spiritual advisors of the people for all time to come. The thickness of their skin shall be Jadahniyeronhkarakeh, seven spans of the hand, that is to say, they shall be genuine proof against angry passions; they are not to take offense at anything that might be said against them, or any wrong that might be perpetrated on them, but that their hearts shall be full of peace and good will; their spirits yearning for the good of their people; long-suffering in carrying out their duties, and their firmness shall be tempered with tenderness. The spirit of anger and fury shall find no lodgement in them, and in all they say and do they shall exercise calmness. And furthermore, in all their deliberations, legislature, or official acts, self shall be entirely cast to oblivion and the general good only of the whole Confederacy sought after; having always in view— not only the present and rising generation, but also the coming generations, all those to come, Onhwhenjakonh Dayekenhsondontye, those whose faces are yet below the surface of the ground, the unborn progeny of the Nation.

Wampum Law: It is provided thus—That should a warrior customarily assist with marked ability and earnestness the Sachems of his nation in council and should he prove himself wise, honest, and trustworthy, the Sachems of the nation may in their discretion give him a seat among the Sachems of the Nation whereof he shall be a member. The Sachems shall then at the next assembly of the Ohkayondentsherah proclaim him a Pine Tree sprung up for them (Pine Tree Chief), the aforesaid Sachems Wahhdihnehdethahseh. Should he ever do anything contrary to the Constitution of the Kayonecyonni, no one has the right to depose him from office, but thereafter everyone shall be deaf to whatever he may say, thus his mouth may be closed. Should he resign his seat in council, no one has the right to present him and he himself has no right to appoint a successor to himself. This class of chiefs is not of the same order as that of the Sachems. In case of the death or resignation of one of this class there shall be no successor to him.

Wampum Law: It is provided thus—That the women of every clan of the Five Nations shall have a council fire which shall ever be burning for the purpose of holding a council of the women of the clan when in their opinion it is necessary for the interest and advantage of the people and their commonwealth. The decisions, conclusions, or recommendations of such a council shall be introduced for consideration into the council of the Confederate Sachems by the War-Chief of that Clan.

Wampum Law: It is provided thus—That the warriors of every clan of the Five Nations shall have a council fire which shall ever be burning for the purpose of holding a council of the warriors of the clan when in their opinion it seems necessary to hold such a council to transact such business as may be needful for the welfare of the clan or the people. It shall have the same rights as the council fire of the women.

Wampum Law: It is provided thus—This shall be constitutional that whenever an important affair be brought before the Five Nations Union Council, something that would tend to have a bad effect on the nation, be disadvantageous to it, something that would ruin their national prosperity, then the union or confederate council of the Sachems must refer the affair to their people in general, who shall have a voice and decide.

Note: Tradition says that the Oneidas were the second nation to agree to follow the Laws of the Great Peace, the Iroquois Constitution, the first United Nations. The Iroquois League set the example of women suffrage, the initiative and referendum, the recall, universal social security, and representative government.

TREATIES CONCERNING THE ONEIDA NATION

Treaty with the Six Nations as regards the Oneida Nation: October 22, 1784, Articles concluded at Fort Stanwix between Oliver Wolcott, Richard Butler, and Arthur Lee, Commissioners Plenipotentiary from the United States, in Congress assembled, on one part, and the Sachems and Warriors of the Six Nations on the other. Article II, the Oneida and Tuscarora Nations shall be secured in the possession of the lands on which they are settled.

Treaty with the Six Nations, January 9, 1789, as regards the Oneida Nation: Articles of a treaty made at Fort Harmar between Arthur St. Clair, Esquire, Governor of the territory of the United States of America, northwest of the river Ohio, and Commissioner Plenipotentiary of the said United States, for removing all controversy, regulating trade, and settling boundaries between the Indian nations in the northern department and the said United States, of the one part, and the sachems and warriors of the Six Nations of the other part: Article 3. The Oneida and Tuscarora Nations, are also again secured and confirmed in the possession of their respective lands.

Treaty with the Six Nations, November 11, 1794, as regards the Oneida Nation: The President of the United States having determined to hold a conference with the Six Nations of Indians for the purpose of removing from their minds all causes of complaint, and establishing a firm and permanent friendship with them; and Timothy Pickering being appointed sole agent for that purpose; and the agent having met and conferred with the Sachems, Chiefs, and Warriors of the Six Nations, in a general council: Now, in order to accomplish the good design of this conference, the parties have agreed on the following articles; which, when ratified by the President, with the advice and consent of the Senate of the United States, shall be binding on them, and the Six Nations. Article II. The United States acknowledge the lands reserved to the Oneida, Onondaga, and Cayuga Nations, in their respective treaties with the State of New York, and called their reservations, to be their property; and the United States will never claim the same, nor disturb them or either of the Six Nations, nor their Indian friends residing thereon and united with them, in the free use and enjoyment thereof; but the said reservations shall remain theirs, until they choose to sell the same to the people of the United States, who have the right to purchase.

Treaty with the Oneidas, December 8, 1794: A treaty between the United States and the Oneida, Tuscarora, and Stockbridge Indians, dwelling in the country of the Oneidas. Whereas, in the late war between Great Britain and the United States of America, a body of the Oneida and Tuscarora and the Stockbridge Indians adhered faithfully to the United States, and assisted them with their warriors; and in consequence of this adherence and assistance the Oneidas and Tuscaroras, at an unfortunate period of the war, were driven from their homes, and their houses were burnt and their property destroyed: And as the United States in the time of their distress, acknowledged their obligations to these faithful friends, and promised to reward them: and the United States being now in a condition to fulfill the promises then made: the following articles are stipulated by the respective parties for that purpose; to be in force when ratified by the President and Senate: Article I: The United States will pay the sum of five thousand dollars, to be distributed among individuals of the Oneida and Tuscarora Nations, as a compensation for their individual losses and services during the late war between Great Britain and the United States. The only man of the Kaughnawaugas now remaining in the Oneida Country, as well as some few very meritorious persons of the Stockbridge Indians, will be considered in the distribution. Article II: For the general accommodation of these Indian Nations residing in the country of the Oneidas, the United States will cause to be erected a complete gristmill and sawmill, in a situation to serve the present principal settlements of these nations. Or if such one convenient situation cannot be found, then the United States will cause to be erected two such gristmills and sawmills in places where it is now known the proposed accommodation may be effected. Of this the United States will judge. Article III: The United States will provide, during three years after the mills shall be completed, for the expense of employing one or two suitable persons to manage the mills, to keep them in repair, to instruct some young men of the three nations in the arts of the miller and sawyer, and to provide teams and utensils for carrying on the work of the mills. Article IV: The United States will provide one thousand dollars to be applied in building a convenient church at Oneida, in the place of the one which was there burnt by the enemy in the late war.

The Oneidas held no fewer than thirty treaties with the State of New York between the years 1788 and 1842.

REQUIKENING ADDRESS
ONENH JATHONDEK, SEWARIHWISAANONGHKWE KAYANERENGH—KOWA

You will recall the words of the Requickening Address at the raising of Hodiyaner, wherein the Sachem sings:

Woe, Woe! Hearken ye! We are diminished, Woe, Woe!

The cleared land has become a thicket—Woe, Woe!

That was the wail of the olden day, but a new day has come even to the People of the Long House, and it is better to chant:

Rejoice and Hearken ye! We have endured!

Rejoice, rejoice!

The thicket has become cleared land—Rejoice, rejoice!

We, the People of the Great League have no time for mourning now, for the past has gone beyond recovery. The present is here and the future awaits our preparation. A new responsibility has come and with it opportunity.

'Tis well to remember the precepts of the ancient day, but it also is well to open our eyes to the new era in which we live today! Mind and spirit must be implemented for the world's endeavor as never before. The future rules us now. The Long House of old was as strong as its individual timbers, and endured the storm of time because each was strong. Today in order to weather the whirlwind of civilization, the character and intelligence of each one of us must stand the test—even as our warriors of gone-by centuries were stalwart, brave, and noble of mind.

Have courage, be strong! No longer are we only of a tribe, a nation, a race, but of humanity. Our highest rights now are to be secured by the full performance of every duty that falls upon us as citizens of one world wherein all men are brothers. In the march of man into the sun of destiny you and I, as members of the Great League, cannot lag behind when duty calls. Our mettle is under test by an appraising

world. This is our challenge, Mohawks! We cannot forget our heritage; it calls upon us to live as Deganahwideh would have had us live beneath the Tree of Peace and obedient to the Kayanerengh-Kowa.

Only by this ancient wisdom will Rawenio give us victory. Let us highly resolve that we shall press forward to win a new place among nations of the earth and then unite with them as members of the common Brotherhood of Man.

Da-nehoh!   GAWASO - WANNEH

THE LAST SPEECH OF
DESKAHEH

Deskaheh was a Cayuga Chief of the Younger Bear Clan and an Iroquois Patriot. Deskaheh was born in 1873 and was installed in the Six Nations Council in 1917. He was, in 1921, appointed Speaker. At Ottawa, London, and Geneva, Switzerland, he defended the right of the Six Nations to live under their own laws on their own lands, and to worship the Creator in their own way. A firm believer in the teachings of Deganawidah, he devoted his whole life to the service of his people. He honored his people and is honored by them.

On the evening of March 10, 1925, suffering from a serious attack of pleurisy and pneumonia, he made his last speech. It was before a radio microphone in Rochester. Once more, and more forcefully than ever, he hurled defiance at the big nations that had disregarded the claims of the Six Nations People.

Nearly everyone who is listening to me is a pale face, I suppose. I am not. My skin is not red but that is what my people are called by others. My skin is brown, light brown, but our cheeks have a little flush and that is why we are called redskins. We don't mind that. There is no difference between us, under the skins, that any expert with a carving knife has ever discovered.

My home is on the Grand River. Until we sold off a large part, our country extended down to Lake Erie, where, 140 winters ago, we had a little seashore of our own and a birch-bark navy. You would call it Canada. We do not. We call the little ten-miles square we have left the "Grand River Country." We have the right to do that. It is ours. We have the written pledge of George III that we should have it forever as against him or his successors and he promised to protect us in it. We didn't think we would ever live long enough to find that a British promise was not good. An enemy's foot is in our country and George V knows it, for I told him so but he will not lift his finger to protect us nor will any of his ministers. One who would take away our rights is of course, our enemy. Do you think that any government should stop to consider whether any selfish end is to be gained or lost in the keeping of its word?

In some respects we are just like you. We like to tell our troubles. You do that. You told us you were in great trouble a few winters ago because a big giant with a big stick was after you. We helped you whip him. May of our young men volunteered and many gave their lives for you. You were very willing to let them fight in the front ranks in France. Now we want to tell our troubles to you—I do not mean that we are calling on your governments. We are tired of calling on the governments of pale-faced peoples in American and in Europe. We have tried that and found it was no use. They deal only in fine words—We want something more than that—We want justice from now on. After all that has happened to us that is not much for us to ask. You got half of your territory here by warfare upon redmen, usually unprovoked, and you got about a quarter of it by bribing their chiefs and not over a quarter of it did you get openly and fairly. You might have gotten a good share of it by fair means if you had tried. You young people of the United States may not believe what I am saying. Do not take my word but read your history. A good deal of true history about that has got into print now. We have a little territory left—just enough to live and die on. Don't you think your governments ought to be ashamed to take that away from us by pretending it is part of theirs? You ought to be ashamed if you let them. Before it is all gone we mean to let you know what your governments are doing. If you are a free people you can have your own way. The governments at Washington and Ottawa have a silent partnership of policy. It is aimed to break up every tribe of redmen so as to dominate every acre of their territory. Your high officials are the nomads today—not the Red People. Your officials won't stay at home. Over in Ottawa they call that policy "Indian advancement." Over in Washington they call it "assimilation." We, who would be the helpless victims, say it is tyranny. If this must go on to the bitter end, we would rather you come with your guns and poison gases and get rid of us that way. Do it openly and above board. Do away with the pretense that you have the right to subjugate us to your will. Your governments do that by enforcing your alien laws upon us. This is an underhanded way. They can subjugate us if they will through the use of your law courts. But how would you like to be dragged down to Mexico, to be tried by Mexicans and jailed under Mexican law for what you do at home?

We want none of your laws or customs that we have not willingly adopted for ourselves. We have adopted many. You have adopted some of ours—votes for women, for instance—We are as well-behaved as you and you would think so if you knew us better. We would be happier today, if left alone, than you who call yourselves Canadians and Americans. We have no jails and do not need them. You have many jails, but do they hold all the criminals you convict? And do you convict or prosecute all your violators of the thousands of laws you have?

Your governments have lately resorted to new practices in their Indian policies. In the old days they often bribed our chiefs to sign treaties to get our lands. Now they know that our remaining territory can easily be gotten away from us by first taking our political rights away, in forcing us into your citizenship. They give jobs in their Indian offices to the bright young people among us who will take them and who, to earn their pay, say that our people wish to become citizens with you and that we are ready to have our tribal life destroyed and want your governments to do it. But this is not true. Your governments of today learned that method from the British. The British have long practiced it on weaker peoples in carrying out their policy of subjugating the world, if they can, to British Imperialism. Under cover of it, your law-makers now assume to govern other peoples too weak to resist your courts. There is no three-mile limits or twelve-mile limits to strong governments who wish to do that. About three winters ago the Canadian government set out to take mortgages on farms of our returned soldiers to secure loans made to them intending to use Canadian courts to enforce those mortgages in the name of Canadian authority within our country. When Ottawa tried that, our people resented it. We knew that would mean the end of our own government. Because we did so, the Canadian government began to enforce all sorts of Dominion and Provincial laws over us and quartered armed men among us to enforce Canadian laws and customs upon

us. We appealed to Ottawa in the name of our right as a separate people and by right of our treaties, and the door was closed in our faces.
We then went to London with our treaty and asked for the protection
it promised and got no attention. Then we went to the League of
Nations at Geneva with its covenant to protect little peoples and to
enforce respect for treaties by its members, and we spend a whole
year patiently waiting but got no hearing.

To punish us for trying to preserve our rights, the Canadian Government has now pretended to abolish our government by Royal
Proclamation and has pretended to set up a Canadian-made government over us, composed of the few traitors among us who are willing
to accept pay from Ottawa and do its bidding. Finally Ottawa officials,
under pretense of a friendly visit, asked to inspect our precious
wampum belts, made by our Fathers centuries ago as records of our
history, and when shown to them, those false-faced officials seized
and carried away those belts as bandits take your precious belongings. The only difference was that our aged wampum-keeper did not
put up his hands. Our hands go up only when we address the Great
Spirit. Yours go up, I hear, only when some one of you is going
through the pockets of his own white brother. According to your
newspapers they are up now a good deal of the time. The Ottawa government thought that with no wampum belts to read in the opening
of our Six Nations Councils, we would give up our home rule and self-
government, the victims of superstition. Any superstition of which
the Grand River People have been victims are not in reverence for
wampum belts, but in their trust in the honor of governments who
boast of a higher civilization.

We entrusted the British, long ago, with large sums of our money
to care for when we ceded back parts of our territory. They took
$140,000 of that money seventy-five winters ago to use for their own
selfish ends, and we have never been able to get it back.

Your government of the United States, I hear, has just decided to
take away the political liberties of all the redmen you promised to
protect forever by passing such a law through your Congress in defiance of the treaties made by George Washington. That law, of course,
would mean the breaking up of the tribes if enforced. Our people

would rather be deprived of their money than their political liberties. So would you.

I suppose some of you never heard of my people before and that many of you, if you ever did, supposed that we were all long gone to our Happy Hunting Grounds. No! There are as many of us as there were a thousand winters ago. There are more of us than there used to be and that makes a great difference in the respect we we get from your governments.

I ask you a question or two. Do not hurry with your answers. Do you believe—really believe—that all peoples are entitled to equal protection of international law now that you are so strong? Do you believe—really believe—that treaty pledges should be kept? Think these questions over and answer them to yourselves.

We are not as dependent in some ways as we were in the early days. We do not need interpreters now. We know your language and can understand your words for ourselves and we have learned to decide for ourselves what is good for us. It is bad for any people to take the advice of an alien people as to that.

You Mothers, I hear, have a good deal to say about your government. Our Mothers have always had a hand in ours. Maybe you can do something to help us now. If you white mothers are hard-hearted and will not, perhaps you boys and girls who are listening and who have loved to read stories about our people—the true ones, I mean—will help us when you grow up, if there are any of us left then to be helped. If you are bound to treat us as though we were citizens under your government then those of your people who are land hungry will get our farms away from us by hooks and crooks under your property laws and in your courts that we do not understand and do not wish to learn. We would then be homeless and have to drift into your big cities to work for wages, to buy bread, and have to pay rent, as you call it, to live on this earth and to live in little rooms in which we would suffocate. We would then be scattered and lost to each other and lost among so many of you. Our boys and girls would then have to intermarry with you or not at all. If consumption took us off or if we brought no children into the world or our blood mixed with the ocean of your blood then there would be no Iroquois left. So boys and girls, if you grow up and claim the right to live together and govern yourselves, and you ought to, and if you do not concede the same right to other peoples, you will be tyrants won't you? If you do not like that word, use a better one if you can find one, but don't deceive yourselves by the word you use.

Boys—you respect your fathers because they are members of a free people and have a voice in the government over them and because they helped to make it and made it for themselves and will hand it down to you. If you knew that your fathers had nothing to do with the government they are under but were mere subjects of other men's wills, you could not look up to them and they could not look you in the face. They would not be real men then. Neither would we. The Fathers among our people have been real men. They cry out now against the injustice of being treated as something else and being called incompetents who must be governed by another people—which means the people who think that way about them. Boys—think this over. Do it before your minds lose the power to grasp the idea that there are other peoples in this world besides your own and with an equal right to be here. You see that a people as strong as yours is a great danger to other peoples near you. Already your will comes pretty near being law in this world where no one can whip you, think then what it will mean if you grow up with a will to be unjust to other peoples; to believe that whatever your government does to other peoples is no crime, however wicked. I hope the Irish-Americans hear that and will think about it—they used to when that shoe pinched their foot.

This is the story of the Mohawks, the story of the Oneidas, of the Cayugas—I am a Cayuga—of the Onondagas, the Senecas, and the Tuscaroras. They are the Iroquois. Tell it to those who have not been listening. Maybe I will be stopped from telling it. But if I am prevented from telling it over, as I hope to do, the story will not be lost. I have already told it to thousands of listeners in Europe—it has gone into the records where your children can find it when I may be dead or be in jail for daring to tell the truth—I have told this story in Switzerland. They have free speech in little Switzerland. One can tell the truth over there in public even if it is uncomfortable for some great people.

This story comes straight from Deskaheh, one of the Chiefs of the Cayugas. I am the speaker of the Council of the Six Nations, the oldest League of Nations now existing. It was founded by Hiawatha. It is a League which is still alive and intends, as best it can, to defend the rights of the Iroquois to live under its own laws in their own little countries now left to them; to worship their Great Spirit in their own way and to enjoy the rights which are as surely theirs as the white man's rights are his own.

If you think the Iroquois are being wronged, write letters from Canada to your ministers of Parliament and from the United States to your congressmen and tell them so. They will listen to you for you elect them. If they are against us, ask them to tell you when and how they got the right to govern people who have no part in your government and do not live in your country, but live in their own. They can't tell you that.

One word, more so that you be sure to remember our people. If it had not been for them, you would not be here. If, one hundred and sixty-six winters ago, our warriors had not helped the British at Quebec, Quebec would not have fallen to the British. The French would then have driven your English-speaking forefathers out of this land, bag and baggage. Then it would have been a French-speaking people here today, not you. That part of your history cannot be blotted out by stealing of our wampum belts in which that is recorded.

I could tell you much more about our people and I may some other time—if you would like to have me.

The next morning after his speech, Deskaheh was ordered by the doctor to a Rochester hospital, as he had a serious attack of pleurisy and pneumonia. He was under treatment at the Homeopathic Hospital for eight weeks, then, the doctors giving him up, Chief Deskaheh asked to be taken back to the Tuscarora Reservation along the banks of the Niagara River where, his face toward his beloved Grand River Country and people, he died on June 27, 1925, mourned by the Iroquois people.

MESSAGE TO THE FOLKS AT HOME

Karithonniennitsera, nonwa wenniserateniron, aonhaa iakoitak-
enhen ne ithotiiosa. Toka karihonnienni ne ononkwehonwe enwaton
eto niiotsi enhotiioten tsiniiot ne ratihnaraken. Nekati teioton-
wsentsiohon ne aiethiretsiaron ne iethiienokonah ne ahonteweienste,
asken nee no rahiatonseraienteri neo enhoioten ne kaiotenseranoron.

Lonkwateriwaienni oni ne aiethiriwawase ne ahonatsteniaronke
ne ahonteweienste onen kine enwaton n senha watiesen tsi enhatit-
senri neensotiioten ne kaiotenseriio. Eto oni nentewe akwekon eniok-
waiaste takenha ne tionkwehonwe.

Kennowa kaien, teiotonwentaiohon oni ne onkwehonwe ne aion-
teweienste ne onkwehonweneha asken, toka ienoronhkwa tsi
iakonkwehonwe iakoriwaien ki ne aionronkhake ne onkwehonweneha.

Otiake ne ontionkweta ratiweientetas ne rennaraken tsinihawen-
natens tanon iah tehonrankha tsinihatiwennotens ne onkwehonwe.
Aetowakwenieseke tosa nonwenton aonteriwanton ne onkwehon-
wenetha tsi tewatatis.

Keniken kahiatonsera, ionkwaretsiarona ne aetowatatiseke ne
tsinitowawennotens, tanon watoken natekaron kento enkahiatonke
niatekonne kariwiios.

Nekate aesowathontatseke ne sowakstenhokonah, aietsirihonnien
ne nithotiionse ne snkwehonweneha, onen kine enwaton enhatiwen-
nahnotaseke tsinahoten enkaiahtonke ne kento.

English Translation For Above

Education is best for every boy and girl in these modern times.
With an education, our young people can hold their place in any
capacity just the same as any white man. We should encourage our
children to get all the education they can while they are young. We
should encourage them to go to school as long as they can because
after they are out of school it is the boy with the best education and

training that gets the best and the easiest job. Every boy and girl will have to work some day and if we parents can help make it easier for them then we are doing the right thing. We should take care of them while they are young and do our best for them then. So let us not discourage them but encourage them to continue school. If they are ready for High School next year then by all means insist that they go to High School next year. If they have the desire and ability to go to College, then send them to College. But for the good of our race, encourage them to get an education. This is the tool that the white man uses to make life easier. This will be a benefit, not only for your children but for yourself in the long run.

It is bad not to know your own language. Indian boys and girls who cannot speak Indian are often ashamed. So, be sure to insist that your children speak and write Indian. Many boys or girls who go to college learn to speak French, German, or other foreign language and it never does them much good. It is easy to learn to speak two or three different languages, so do not allow your children to grow up without a knowledge of their own tongue. We wish every child to learn to speak good English but also want them to learn to speak Indian. Our language must be kept alive.

WHERE THE IROQUOIS ARE TODAY

The League of the Five Nations (Six Nations after 1722) formerly inhabited New York State from the Hudson River to Lake Erie. Today several bands of Six Nations Iroquois live on small reservations in several parts of the United States as well as in Canada.

The Six Nations have a treaty with the government of the United States which gives them the status of an independent protectorate of the United States. This is called, "The Treaty of 1784." It was confirmed and added to autonomy. The title of the original territory was vested in them. The United States absolutely guaranteed to these Indians protection for all time to come. The Six Nations Indians of Canada have a similar treaty with Great Britain, "The Haldimand Treaty." Though a white man boundary line separates the United States and Canada, it does not affect the Six Nations who have a political relationship with each other. There is no Canadian or American boundary line for Six Nations Indians who, as Native Americans, were given in a solemn treaty, the Jay Treaty, the right to cross and recross the imaginary line unmolested and free of duty.

The Six Nation Country, Ohsweken, on which live Iroquois of all the Six Nations as well as several other tracts protected by the Six Nations, occupy a tract of land situated along the Grand River of Ontario, Canada. This land was settled by the Six Nations in the year 1784, for services rendered Great Britain. They were promised this land in the Haldimand Treaty forever. The Six Nation Country today contains 43,696 acres of land.

The Akwesasne St. Regis Reservation is in the north part of New York State. It covers 16,640 acres of land on the American side of the reservation and 7384 acres of land on the Canadian side. The St. Regis Indians are mostly Mohawks. The Mohawks are the best basket makers east of the Mississippi River. They and their Mohawk brethren of Kahnawake are also known as the best steel workers in the world. Their reservation, formed on Mohawk territory, was settled in 1759.

In 1667 a band of Mohawks residing in the Mohawk Valley, under the influence of Roman Catholic missionaries, migrated to Canada.

They now live along the banks of the St. Lawrence River opposite the city of Montreal. Their reservation, Kahnawake, contains 12,000 acres of land.

On the Bay of Quinte, Lake Ontario, near the city of Deseronto, is Tyendinaga Mohawk Reservation. It contains about 17,000 acres of land. This reservation was formed in the year 1784 by Indians of the Mohawk Valley.

The Indians of the Two Mountain (Kanesatake) or Oka Reservation are mostly Mohawks. Their small reservation along the Ottawa River, west of Montreal, Quebec, was formed around the year 1721.

The Gibson (Watha) Mohawk Reservation is near Bala, Georgian Bay, Ontario. The Mohawk band there migrated west from the Oka Mohawk Reservation after being, they say, swindled out of most of their reservation by Christian missionaries.

A small band of Mohawks, known as Paul's Band, migrated to the far west during the year 1804. They were Mohawk voyageurs. They settled along the Athabasca River on the Michel Reservation near Edmonton, Alberta.

In spite of the fact that the Oneida Indians fought for the Americans during the Revolutionary War and saved Washington's starving army at Valley Forge by giving them several hundred bushels of corn, the Oneida Nation fared little better than did the Cayuga Nation. Their original beautiful country has been narrowed down to one very small reservation of a little over thirty acres of land. A small part of the Oneida Nation refused, in spite of many threats, to leave their homes and have remained near the seat of their ancient Council Fire. These few live near Oneida Castle in New York State. A few Oneidas live on the Onondaga Reservation in New York State and with the Six Nation People of Ohsweken, Ontario, Canada. A portion of the Oneida Nation moved to the Thames River in Ontario, where they now live on a reservation called Muncey. This reservation contains 4,600 acres of land.

In 1821, through the greediness of white people, many Oneidas were moved west to what is now the state of Wisconsin. This was done in direct violation of their most sacred treaty between that nation and the Thirteen Colonies. This Oneida Band settled along the banks of

Green Bay on Lake Michigan. Though the Green Bay Oneidas were given the promise that their Wisconsin land was to be theirs forever, they do not have a reservation today. Their country, by the use of threat and force and against their wishes, was allotted to others. Though they are somewhat scattered, they still have an Indian settlement called Oneida.

Not far from the city of Syracuse in New York State, in the center of the ancient country of the Iroquois, is the small Onondaga Reservation. This reservation embraces 6,100 acres of hilly land. Onondaga, in conjunction with Six Nation Onondagas, as in ancient days, still furnishes the Firekeepers of the Iroquois Confederacy.

Through the greediness of the white settlers, who wanted their beautiful country, the Cayuga Nation lost its reservation. Many of the Cayuga, believing false promises, migrated to Kansas where they died of disease and starvation. A small group returned and were welcomed and given shelter by the Senecas. On the Cattaraugus Reservation several Cayuga families reside. There are also a few who live at Allegheny and Tonawands. A portion of the nation moved to Green Bay, Wisconsin. Another large group moved to the Six Nation Country along the Grand River. Still another group was driven west of the Mississippi River where they live with a band of Senecas in Oklahoma. They still retain their national name and linage. The Cayuga chiefs and people are trying to secure a small portion of their former home along Lake Cayuga, a spot that they can call home.

The Cayuga and Seneca Indians of Oklahoma live on a reservation in Ottawa County, located in the eastern section of the Indian State. Before and after the Revolutionary War the Senecas established colonies in what is now the state of Ohio. They were called the "Senecas of Sandusky." Along with these were a few Tuscaroras, Cayugas, Mohawks, and Onondagas. In 1831 the United States, under President Jackson, forced these people to move west to Indian Territory, now the state of Oklahoma. Their forced journey was a sad and difficult one, and many died during the long trip. On July 4, 1832, after six months of travel, these people arrived at the Elk River in Indian Territory, where they now reside. Later a band of Cayuga Indians from Canada joined them and there they live at the present time.

The Cattaraugus Reservation, near Gowanda, New York, contains 26,680 acres of land. The Cattaraugus people are Seneca Indians. Living with them are several families of Cayuga Indians. Cattaraugus Reservation land is very good farm land and it is also valuable because of the oil and gas found there.

The Allegheny Seneca Reservation stretches 40 miles along the Allegheny River in the southwestern part of New York State. This reservation contains 30,469 acres of land. This includes the city of Salamanca and five small white villages. The Seneca Nation also includes the Cornplanter Reservation, a small reservation that contains 640 acres of land in northwestern Pennsylvania.

The Tonawanda Senecas left the main band of Senecas in the year 1848. They bought land near the city of Akron, New York. Their reservation covers 7,549 acres of land. Living with them are several families of Cayuga Indians.

The Tuscarora are an Iroquoian Nation originally living where the state of North Carolina is now located. It is recorded that they welcomed and fed the early explorers from Europe when they came to the country of the Tuscaroras. However, after the whites had increased in numbers, they reached out and demanded the country of the Tuscaroras. The Tuscaroras were also in great demand by the whites as slaves to work in the tobacco fields. Because of their grievances, these people fought the white settlers but were defeated and driven from their homes. They petitioned the Five Nation Confederacy for protection and a seat in the Iroquois Country. The Confederacy granted their request and they were given land by the Oneidas. This land was the territory between the Unadilla and the Chenango Rivers in what is now central New York State. Later they migrated west to the banks of Lake Ontario. There the Seneca Nation gave them land. This, along with 4,329 acres of land that they themselves bought, make up their present reservation. Later the Tuscarora became the sixth nation of the Iroquois Confederacy.

Today many Six Nations people live in cities away from the reservations.

BOOKS BY
TEHANETORENS

(RAY FADDEN)

Legends of the Iroquois
by Tehanetorens
$9.95 USA
$14.95 Canada

Wampum Belts of the
Iroquois
by Tehanetorens
$9.95 USA
$14.95 Canada

Sacred Song of the
Hermit Thrush
by Tehanetorens
$5.95 USA—$8.95 Canada

Available from your local bookstore or from:

**Book Publishing Company
PO Box 99
Summertown, TN 38483**
1-800-695-2241
Please include $3.00 per book additional for shipping.

These important Native American books
are available from your local bookstore.

Chants and Prayers
$9.95—$14.95 Canada

Dream Feather
$11.95—$17.95 Canada

Seven Clans
of the
Cherokee
$4.95—$7.95
Canada

How Can One Sell the Air?
$6.95—$10.95 Canada

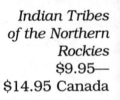

Indian Tribes
of the Northern
Rockies
$9.95—
$14.95 Canada

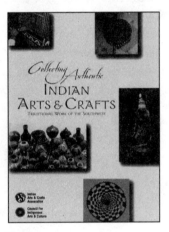

Collecting Authentic
Indian Arts & Crafts
$16.95—$25.95 Canada

Also available from:
Book Publishing Company
PO Box 99
Summertown, TN 38483
1-800-695-2241
Please include $3.00 per book additional for shipping.